The Cyber Resilience Handbook

Defend, prepare, survive

The Cyber Resilience Handbook

Defend, prepare, survive

ANDREW PATTISON

GRCSolutions

GRC Solutions
Unit 3, Clive Court
Bartholomew's Walk
Cambridgeshire Business Park
Ely, Cambridgeshire
CB7 4EA
United Kingdom
www.itgovernance.co.uk

First published in the United Kingdom in 2025 by GRC Solutions.

ISBN 978-1-78778-585-4

Cover image originally sourced from Adobe Stock.

ABOUT THE AUTHOR

Andrew Pattison is the Global Head of GRC and PCI Consultancy at IT Governance, a GRC Solutions company. With a career stretching back to the mid-1990s, Andrew has worked extensively in information security, risk management and business continuity. He is currently supporting several major international organisations implement robust governance and risk approaches for the use and development of AI. He holds an MSc in Information Systems Management, is a certified auditor, and is accredited with both CISM® and CRISC® certifications. Alongside his consultancy work, Andrew has delivered comprehensive training across multiple GRC disciplines, including DORA, NIS, NIST, ISO/IEC 27001, business continuity, CRISC and CISM.

ACKNOWLEDGEMENTS

I would like to thank Stuart Griffin, Technical Writer at IT Governance, a GRC Solutions Company, for his help with the production of this book.

CONTENTS

Contents

INTRODUCTION

In a world increasingly dependent on digital technologies, the need for effective cyber security has never been clearer. Cyber attacks, data breaches, supply chain compromises and technological disruptions have become part of the complex landscape in which we operate, and we greet news stories describing yet another data breach or security failure on the part of organisations that play key roles in our daily lives with wearied stoicism.

For organisations, the emphasis has long been on prevention – building defences and safeguards to stop an attacker from achieving their goals. Yet even the best prepared organisation has weaknesses that an attacker can exploit, and when those defences inevitably fail, many are left scrabbling through long-outdated disaster recovery plans and restoration procedures – if they have them at all.

Simple defence is no longer enough. It is imperative to not only defend against attacks but also properly prepare for the eventuality that one succeeds. The combination of information security and business continuity in defending against and responding to cyber attacks is called 'cyber resilience'.

Cyber resilience goes beyond traditional information and cyber security, which focus on prevention and detection, and embraces a broader, more strategic approach that ensures that systems, networks and the organisations that rely on them can continue to function when adversity strikes. Effective cyber resilience requires a culture of preparedness that considers risk management and recovery planning to be at least as important as cyber defences.

This book will explore the core principles of cyber resilience and explain how you can use ISO 27001 and ISO 22301 to implement a cyber resilience programme in your organisation. By the end of the book, you will understand how to implement both standards and combine them to form an effective, integrated system that will both enhance cyber security and ensure your organisation can respond effectively to a cyber attack or disruption.

CHAPTER ONE: WHAT IS CYBER RESILIENCE?

Most readers will probably be familiar with cyber security – the process of protecting information and digital assets against attack – but cyber resilience goes much further.

It begins with the assumption that a successful attack will occur. This is more likely than you might think – the 2025 UK National Cyber Security Centre (NCSC)'s Cyber Security Breaches Survey found that 43% of businesses reported a cyber security breach or attack in the preceding 12 months.[1]

Once an attack occurs, traditional cyber security is of remarkably little help. Its primary focus is on preventing attacks rather than responding to them, and many of the defensive measures it recommends play no immediate role in recovering systems or maintaining minimum service levels while the attack is underway. Recovery often proceeds in a haphazard, reactive manner as a mix of personnel attempt to contain the damage and restore functionality, with consequent impacts on efficiency, effectiveness and service availability.

Cyber resilience attempts to redress this imbalance. It encompasses detective and preventive measures – cyber security – while placing equal emphasis on responding to

---

[1] UK Government Department for Science, Innovation and Technology, *Cyber Breaches Survey 2025*, June 2025, https://www.gov.uk/government/statistics/cyber-security-breaches-survey-2025/cyber-security-breaches-survey-2025.

and recovering from attacks and delivering key services (even if at reduced capacity) during a disruption. At its core, cyber resilience consists of four principles:

1. Manage and protect
2. Identify and detect
3. Respond and recover
4. Govern and assure

Manage and protect

The manage and protect principle closely corresponds with traditional cyber security. It is focused on understanding the organisation's risk environment, identifying and evaluating risks, and taking action to mitigate them. It should define the core policies that govern the use of IT systems within the organisation and the responsibilities and authorities necessary to ensure effective oversight. It should also lay the foundation for managing IT and information assets across the organisation and deploying core cyber security controls such as identity and access control, malware protection, configuration and patch management, competence and training, and physical and environmental security.

Identify and detect

This principle is focused on monitoring your networks and systems to detect anomalies and potential attacks as early as possible. This relies in part on successful application of the first category, as you must have a clear understanding of your networks, assets and systems to be able to monitor them effectively.

Like the manage and protect principle, much of the actions associated with this principle fall within the realm of cyber security. These include use of security information and event management (SIEM) systems, keeping and monitoring logs and network traffic, tracking potential security events, and auditing physical security measures such as CCTV and visitor entry records.

Respond and recover

The respond and recover principle corresponds with business continuity. It focuses on the actions needed to respond to incidents and attacks effectively, and on ensuring that a specified minimum service level is maintained during a disruption or an incident.

This principle emphasises identifying risks to business and service continuity, developing incident response and business continuity solutions that can be used to respond to incidents, developing formal plans to manage incidents, assigning recovery thresholds and timescales for critical functions and services, and testing plans to ensure they remain effective over time.

Govern and assure

This principle is focused on implementing and maintaining the cyber resilience programme, and ensuring it meets all necessary requirements. Implementing and maintaining cyber resilience effectively requires a governance structure with clearly assigned responsibilities and authorities, management support, resources and continual improvement measures to ensure that the programme remains effective over time.

The programme should be supported by periodic reviews of relevant legislation to ensure that your systems and recovery solutions do not breach applicable requirements; audits and monitoring to ensure that controls and solutions function as expected; and management reviews to ensure the programme continues to align with the organisation's goals.

For organisations that implement their cyber resilience programme by using nationally or internationally recognised standards, this principle also includes achieving and maintaining accredited certification as a marker of assurance for clients and partners.

Cyber resilience vs. disaster recovery

Disaster recovery as a discipline began in the 1970s as a response to increasing dependency on IT systems. Initially, its primary focus was on restoring backups and getting systems back online and rarely considered the organisational impacts of extended downtime, service disruption and related factors.

As IT systems evolved and the risks posed to organisations by significant disruptions (whether cyber or otherwise) became more significant, disaster recovery gradually split into two disciplines: one focused on restoring ICT systems in a largely technical sense, which is still referred to as disaster recovery, and another focused on ensuring the business could maintain at least a minimum degree of operating capacity during a disruptive event, which became known as business continuity management.

In 2003, the British Standards Institute (BSI) published Publicly Available Specification (PAS) 56: *Guide to*

Business Continuity Management. This was followed by a formal standard, BS 25999-1 *Business Continuity Management: Code of Practice*, in 2006.

BS 25999 would eventually be withdrawn in favour of a new standard based on BS 25999 but developed by the International Organization for Standardization (ISO). ISO 22301: *Societal security — Business continuity management systems — Requirements* was first published in 2012. ISO 22301 is used by organisations of all types and sizes to ensure effective business continuity, and its most recent edition is ISO 22301:2019.

The increasing prevalence and complexity of IT systems and the security issues associated with them (which often play a role in IT disruptions) relegated disaster recovery to one of many components necessary to ensure effective cyber security. This natural progression aligned with the increasing global focus on cyber and information security that followed various major cyber attacks and incidents affecting well-known organisations throughout the late 1990s and 2000s.

1995 saw the publication of BS 7799 *Code of Practice for Information Security Management*, a formal methodology for information security based on an internal methodology developed by the Shell corporation. Updated in 1999 to become a two-part standard, BS 7799-1 contained a list of information security controls that would later be adopted by ISO as ISO 27002 *Information technology — Security techniques — Code of practice for information security management*, while BS 7799-2 defined a specification for an information security management system (ISMS) that would deploy and manage those controls – adopted as ISO

27001:2005 *Information technology — Security techniques — Code of practice for information security management.*

ISO 27001 and 27002 underwent further revisions in 2013 and 2022, but a common theme through all three versions is a formal, risk-based approach to managing information security that explicitly defines information security incident management and information security continuity as core controls. The ISO 27000-series has since become an internationally recognised family of standards used by thousands of organisations around the world.

Why cyber resilience and not disaster recovery? Because cyber resilience is a holistic, whole-organisation approach to managing information security and responding effectively to IT incidents, while disaster recovery is merely one part of that approach. Like any single component of a greater whole deployed in isolation, its effectiveness will necessarily be limited.

Defence in depth

One of the key concepts underpinning cyber resilience is defence in depth. This refers to the practice of 'layering' defences so that if one layer is breached, the subsequent layers can still prevent the attacker from achieving their goal.

For example, user access control (UAC) prevents attackers gaining entry to your systems without login information. However, if an attacker does obtain login information (e.g. via a phishing attack), they can access your systems and potentially compromise the entire organisation. A defence-in-depth approach to this problem might be to apply the principle of least privilege (under which users are only given the permissions they need to do their job and no more) to limit the harm an attacker could cause if they do gain access. Another option might be to deploy an AI-enhanced security information and event management (SIEM) system that could detect unusual user traffic and alert administrators in real time.

A true defence-in-depth approach would be to combine all three measures – UAC, least privilege and SIEM systems. How far you go with defence in depth should be governed by risk assessment – there is often little value in adding extra defences for minor risks – and by the impact on cost and resources of your chosen controls. Finding the right balance between cost and protection can be challenging, but it is an essential skill for anyone involved in risk management.

Cyber resilience and operational resilience

It is worth noting that cyber resilience is a subset of a broader concept: operational resilience. Operational resilience is the ability of an organisation to continue to deliver core operations during a disruptive event. While cyber resilience is focused on information security and ICT product or service delivery, operational resilience focuses on being able to ensure delivery of critical services such as power, water, industrial control systems, medical services and other functions essential to daily life.

In recent years, regulators have emphasised the need for effective operational resilience in sectors that are considered 'critical infrastructure', as the degree of interconnectedness between these organisations (and society's reliance on them) means that a disruptive event could have far-reaching effects. A major disruption to Visa's payment systems, or to power or water supplies at a national level, for example, could have serious consequences.

Operational resilience is not the subject of this book. However, should you choose to examine operational resilience as a discipline, you will find a great deal of crossover with many of the things discussed here, particularly those related to ISO 22301. You might also consider reviewing ISO 22316:2017 *Security and resilience — Organizational resilience — Principles and attributes* for further information.

Legislation

Governments across the globe are taking steps to address cyber and operational resilience at the regulatory level. In the EU, the Digital Operational Resilience Act (DORA), which took effect in January 2025, is explicitly focused on ensuring that the financial sector achieves cyber resilience. It requires financial entities to (among other things) develop a documented IT risk management framework and incident management process, and to manage IT third-party risk. Managing IT third-party risk means that DORA extends beyond the financial sector, as in-scope financial organisations will need to ensure their IT suppliers meet the necessary requirements.

Another EU regulation worthy of mention is the second Network and Information Systems Directive (NIS 2). Building on the original EU NIS Directive, NIS 2 is focused on securing critical infrastructure and essential services such as energy and water, key digital services such as payment processing and banking, and core societal services such as postal services, waste management and manufacturing of chemicals, medical devices and food.

NIS 2 requires in-scope organisations to take *"appropriate and proportionate technical, operational and organisational measures to manage the risks posed to the security of network and information systems [used] for their operations or for the provision of their services, and to prevent or minimise the impact of incidents on recipients of their services and on other services".*[2] These measures must include risk management, supply chain security, business continuity and incident management/reporting processes.

The EU has also expanded the scope of its resilience legislation to apply to consumer products. The EU Cyber Resilience Act applies to manufacturers and retailers and requires that the cyber security of products with a 'digital element' is ensured throughout the product's life cycle – including that products *"protect the availability of essential and basic functions, also after an incident, including through resilience and mitigation measures against denial-of-service attacks".*[3] Although the Act itself entered into force on 10 December 2024, most of the provisions take effect in December 2027.

---

[2] European Commission, Directive (EU) 2022/2555 (NIS 2), Article 21 (1), December 2022, *https://eur-lex.europa.eu/eli/dir/2022/2555*.

[3] European Commission, Regulation 2024/2847 (Cyber Resilience Act) Annex I (2) (H), October 2024, *https://eur-lex.europa.eu/legal-content/EN/TXT/?uri=CELEX%3A32024R2847*.

The Act requires compliant products to bear the CE mark and introduces an obligation for manufacturers to report 'actively exploited' vulnerabilities affecting in-scope products to EU cyber security incident response teams (CSIRTs) within 24 hours of discovery. Notably, the law also provides for members of the public to report vulnerabilities (exploited or otherwise) for in-scope products to CSIRTs, who will then inform the manufacturer. In such cases, the CSIRT is likely to require them to resolve the vulnerability in line with the cyber security requirements laid out in Annex I of the Act.

In the UK, the NIS Regulations 2018 implements the provisions of the first EU NIS Directive into UK law, applying the same cyber security and resilience requirements to UK operators of essential services (OES) and digital service providers (DSPs). In short, as with NIS 2, in-scope organisations must implement appropriate and proportionate technical, operational and organisational measures to ensure cyber security and report any 'significant' or 'substantial' incident to the competent authority.

A UK Cyber Security and Resilience Bill is (as of early 2025) also planned.[4] While there is some degree of uncertainty as to the specific measures the bill will contain, it is likely to take a similar approach to the EU's NIS 2

---

[4] UK government Department for Science, Innovation and Technology, *Collection: Cyber Security and Resilience Bill*, September 2024, *https://www.gov.uk/government/collections/cyber-security-and-resilience-bill*

Directive, expanding the scope of requirements to encompass more industries.

In the United States, the New York Department of Financial Services (NYDFS) implemented an amendment to 23 NYCRR Part 500 focused on cyber resilience in November 2023. Effective as of 29 April 2024, it requires in-scope organisations to implement vulnerability management and periodic penetration testing, and to improve asset management and end-of-life (EOL) data management.[5]

At the federal level, the Commodity Futures Trading Commission (CFTC) proposed an operational resilience framework in 2023, which would require affected entities to develop risk management programmes and implement business continuity and disaster recovery plans.[6] At the time of writing, this rule has yet to be finalised – but the direction of travel is clear.

In Canada, organisations that bid on or work for Canadian government defence contracts will need to achieve one of three levels of cyber security certification, with a phased

---

[5] New York Department of Financial Services (NYDFS), *Second Amendment to 23 NYCRR 500*, October 2023, https://www.dfs.ny.gov/system/files/documents/2023/10/rf_fs_2amend2 3NYCRR500_text_20231101.pdf.

[6] Commodity Futures Trading Commission, *Operational Resilience Framework for Futures Commission Merchants, Swap Dealers, and Major Swap Participants*, February 2024, https://www.federalregister.gov/documents/2024/02/26/2024-03826/operational-resilience-framework-for-futures-commission-merchants-swap-dealers-and-major-swap.

rollout beginning in March 2025.[7] Alongside this, the Canadian government is consulting on an amendment to the Telecommunications Act (Bill C-26, or the Critical Cyber Systems Protection Act (CCSPA)) that would take steps to protect critical cyber systems in a similar vein to the EU NIS Directives.[8]

---

[7] Government of Canada, *Cyber security certification for defence suppliers in Canada*, April 2025, *https://www.canada.ca/en/public-services-procurement/services/industrial-security/security-requirements-contracting/cyber-security-certification-defence-suppliers-canada.html*.

[8] Public Safety Canada, *Parliamentary Committee Notes: Q&A - Critical Cyber Systems Protection Act*, March 2025, *https://www.publicsafety.gc.ca/cnt/trnsprnc/brfng-mtrls/prlmntry-bndrs/20250226-1/07-en.aspx*.

CHAPTER TWO: ACHIEVING CYBER RESILIENCE

Achieving cyber resilience is a laudable goal that every organisation should aim for. The question then arises – how to do it? Most organisations already have some degree of cyber security in place, but few have developed serious business continuity measures, and fewer still have combined the two into a managed resilience framework.

To make matters worse, while there are many frameworks that cover specific components of cyber resilience, there is no single 'off-the-shelf' cyber resilience methodology that an organisation can simply pick up and apply. Even if there were, it would likely be too restrictive for some organisations and not restrictive enough for others. Instead, organisations must find their own path to resilience – and in so doing, often end up with a haphazard mix of cyber security measures, untested and ineffective recovery plans, and wasted resources.

The most straightforward way to implement cyber resilience is to consider existing, compatible frameworks that can be deployed together and that align with the four principles that underpin an effective cyber resilience programme. While there are many frameworks to choose from, two lend themselves best to the task at hand: ISO 27001 and ISO 22301.

ISO 27001

ISO 27001 is an international standard for information security management. It defines the specification for an information security management system (ISMS) – a structured approach to managing information security across an organisation.

An ISO 27001-compliant ISMS takes a vendor- and technology-neutral approach to managing information security, focusing on securing the confidentiality, integrity and availability of information (sometimes referred to as the 'CIA triad'). It addresses the 'three pillars of information security' – people, processes and technology – and emphasises the need for top management oversight and direction from the outset. It also contains a list of 93 core information security controls categorised into 4 themes, which taken together form an effective security baseline that can be applied based on the risks faced by the organisation.

The version of ISO 27001 referred to in this book is ISO 27001:2022 *Information security, cybersecurity and privacy protection — Information security management systems — Requirements*.

ISO 22301

Like its counterpart, ISO 22301 defines the specification for a business continuity management system (BCMS) – a structured system to manage business continuity in a similar manner to the way an ISMS manages information security.

An ISO 22301-compliant BCMS is also vendor- and technology-neutral, and focuses on understanding the potential disruptions the organisation might face, determining the potential impact of those disruptions, and developing strategies, solutions and plans that will allow the organisation to manage the disruption and maintain at least a minimum level of capacity while it is being resolved.

Like ISO 27001, ISO 22301 places a similar degree of emphasis on top management oversight and responsibility, and many core components such as continual improvement, management review, internal audits, support and planning are shared with ISO 27001.

The version of ISO 22301 referred to in this book is ISO 22301:2019 *Security and resilience — Business continuity management systems — Requirements.*

An integrated management system

As both standards are developed by ISO, they adhere to ISO's common format for management system standards (known as 'Annex SL'). All ISO management system standards developed on this basis share many of the same clauses, components and terminology, which means that any two or more standards can be combined to create an 'integrated management system' (IMS).

An IMS allows you to operate multiple management systems while minimising duplicated work and resources. Functions that are common to all ISO management systems such as management review, audit, leadership, improvement and other requirements can be shared, reducing costs and making more productive use of project resources. An IMS can also be expanded to encompass additional ISO management systems if future business needs require it.

All ISO management system standards take a risk-based approach. This means that the standards expect that the systems and controls you put in place to mitigate a given risk are proportionate to that risk. This allows each organisation to select and apply controls in a manner commensurate to the risk, but also to their operations and budget, providing useful flexibility.

In a similar manner, many of the information security controls listed in ISO 27001 specify what must be achieved without specifying how the organisation should achieve it. Control A.7.2 on physical entry controls, for example, requires that secure areas are protected by appropriate entry controls and access points, but does not state what those entry controls should be or how they should be used.

As this book is focused on achieving cyber resilience by implementing ISO 27001 and ISO 22301, references that are specific to one of the two standards will refer to the relevant management system (ISMS or BCMS). When discussing the integrated management system, the book will refer to the 'management system' or the IMS.

A quick note on documented information

Both ISO 27001 and ISO 22301 refer to 'documented information' in various clauses. Documented information means documentation that is formally controlled, usually through version numbering, ownership records and other means, so that it is easy to determine if the document in use is the appropriate (usually latest) version. The specific requirements for documented information can be found in Clause 7.5 of both standards.

Some clauses require the organisation to maintain documented information as evidence. For example, both standards require the organisation to define the scope of the management system and maintain that scope as documented information. This usually takes the form of a scope statement or other formal document, and it is controlled as documented information because it is an important part of how the management system is defined.

CHAPTER THREE: IMPLEMENTING CYBER RESILIENCE

Project initiation and buy-in

For any major business project, it is essential that top management understands the need for it and commits to providing the resources necessary to achieve it. A cyber resilience programme, however, needs more than just passive approval to be effective. Top management will be expected to take ultimate responsibility for the programme, drive it forward through its leadership and take an active role in its ongoing development.

If you are responsible for implementing the programme, you will need to ensure that top management understands its role, particularly with respect to ongoing governance and oversight. This doesn't mean that top management must all become cyber security experts (their role is oversight, not technical implementation), but they should have a broad, high-level understanding of the cyber resilience risks the organisation faces and of what ISO 27001 and ISO 22301 are, including their responsibilities with respect to leadership, management review, attending certification body audits (if applicable) and driving improvement.

Context, leadership and scope

Context of the organisation

The first clause shared between both standards, Clause 4, focuses on the context of the organisation. Both standards expect you to determine internal and external issues that are relevant to the organisation's purpose, and which may affect the organisation's ability to achieve the intended outcomes of the ISMS or BCMS (or in this case, the IMS).

This requirement isn't intended to simply state the obvious – these clauses are meant to drive analysis of the conditions that the organisation operates within to ensure they don't adversely affect the organisation or its IMS. You will need to consider factors relevant to cyber security, business continuity and cyber resilience at all levels of the organisation. It may be easier initially to tackle each subject separately, but some crossover is inevitable.

'Internal issues' could include the products or services the organisation offers (including any requirements that they must adhere to), employees and unions, the culture and values of the organisation, the systems, software and networks it uses, operational and development priorities, service uptime requirements, governance concerns, and more.

'External issues' can include legal and regulatory requirements, risks and opportunities in the supply chain, media and communications, the environment in which the organisation operates (whether financial, operational, etc.), relevant technological changes and advancements (e.g. AI), and other external factors.

This process isn't just focused on issues that might result in a negative impact. You should also consider opportunities that could lead to a positive outcome. The outcome of the exercise (perhaps in the form of a SWOT or PESTLE analysis) will inform both the scope of the IMS and the policies, processes and controls that comprise it.

Neither standard asks that you formally document the internal and external issues you identify. Despite this, it may be sensible to do so, if only so that you have something you can show to an external auditor.

Interested parties

The next step is to determine the needs and expectations of interested parties. These are anyone with an interest in the functioning of the IMS and are commonly also referred to as 'stakeholders'.

To begin, first identify the interested parties that are relevant to the IMS. As with the context of the organisation, it may be easier and more effective to identify parties relevant to the ISMS and BCMS separately. The list might include customers, suppliers, regulators, employees, unions or other groups that are affected by, or that can affect, the IMS.

Once you have a complete list, the next step is to identify their requirements. Most of the examples provided will require that you protect the information you hold and comply with applicable laws regarding its use, while customers and partners will require that the products or services you provide are available when needed and not subject to extended periods of disruption. Your suppliers will require that you adhere to any relevant contractual obligations, and employees will require that you pay their wages on time.

It may be easier to conduct this as a two-part exercise, focusing first on requirements that have some relation to cyber security and then on requirements relevant to business continuity and resilience. Once you have identified all requirements, the next step is to consider which of them will be addressed through the IMS. Requirements related to protecting data and recovering from disruptions will naturally need to be addressed through the IMS, but you should carefully examine the implications of other requirements in case they also need to be accounted for in the IMS.

Under ISO 22301, there is an additional sub-clause that requires the organisation to develop a documented process to identify legal and regulatory requirements relevant to the continuity of its products, services and activities, to ensure any such requirements are accounted for within the IMS, and to document the outputs and keep them up to date.

ISO 27001, on the other hand, assumes that legal and regulatory requirements relevant to the cyber security of the organisation and its products and services will be identified as part of the main exercise to identify the requirements of interested parties. It has no requirement to document the process or keep records, but as you will need both to comply with ISO 22301, there is no harm (and some value) in extending the remit of the process and records to account for legal and regulatory requirements relevant to both standards.

The goal of this exercise is to identify interested parties and their requirements as these directly feed into other aspects of the IMS. Avoid the temptation to extend the exercise to consider risks and opportunities associated with these parties and their requirements – that step will follow later.

Scope

Unlike much of the combined IMS, the scope is one area in which each standard must be tackled individually. Both ISO 27001 and ISO 22301 require that you define and document the scope of the management system by developing a scope statement that defines the boundaries within which it will operate.

It is very important that you define the scope clearly and carefully for each management system, as the scope forms the basis for certification. You can develop separate scope statements for each management system (perhaps with an accompanying statement that explains how they work as a single system) or combine both statements into a single document.

Both standards require that you consider the internal and external issues you identified under Clause 4.1 and the interested parties and requirements identified under Clause 4.2 when determining the scope. In addition:

- ISO 27001 requires that you consider the interfaces and dependencies between tasks performed by your organisation and tasks performed by other organisations (e.g. suppliers, Cloud services), as these interfaces are frequently a source of cyber risk.
- ISO 22301 requires that you consider the organisation's mission, goals, obligations, location,

size, nature and complexity when defining the scope, and that you identify products and services that are within scope.

The scope of each management system (and in turn, the IMS) can only comprise functions within the management authority of your organisation. Outsourced processes can be included, but the organisations that perform those processes are not under your authority and therefore cannot be part of the scope.

The ISMS scope statement should clearly define the logical (i.e. networks and systems) and physical boundaries to which it will apply. The BCMS scope should clearly define the products, services and parts of the business that it applies to. For a cyber resilience programme, the scope of the BCMS should be limited to the products, services, systems and associated business areas within the remit of the programme, and so coverage will likely be very similar to that of the ISMS scope.[9]

Exclusions from the scope of either standard must be justified and documented. ISO 22301 requires that exclusions do *"not affect the organisation's ability and*

---

[9] The scope of the BCMS can be expanded beyond the remit of the cyber resilience programme if you choose to do so, and there are certainly benefits in taking such an approach. However, if you are approaching cyber resilience or the standards for the first time, we strongly advise implementing the cyber resilience programme first. This will minimise confusion, limit scope overreach and make for a smoother implementation process. Once implemented (and, if applicable, certified), allow time for the IMS to bed in (e.g. 1–2 years) and only then consider extending its scope.

responsibility to provide business continuity, as indicated by business impact assessment or risk assessment and applicable legal requirements".[10] This means that you can't exclude a part of the business if doing so would undermine your ability to ensure business continuity in parts of the business that are in scope (or if doing so would breach related legal requirements).

Both standards require that the scope is treated as documented information. You should also ensure that the scope statement is stored in an accessible format (e.g. .doc or .pdf), as external auditors will refer to it during surveillance audits.

ISMS/BCMS

The final part of Clause 4 in both standards requires that you *"establish, implement, maintain and continually improve"* the management system, its processes and their interactions. This clause is included partly so that there is an explicit requirement to implement the ISMS or BCMS in line with the standard, but also to emphasise the need to implement and maintain the processes and interactions that support their operation.

All management systems (and all business operations more generally) rely on processes to function. It is therefore always in the best interests of the organisation that its processes are clear, practical, well documented and kept up to date. This may seem like stating the obvious, but for many organisations this remains an afterthought. All too

---

[10] ISO 22301:2019 Clause 4.3.2.

often, auditors encounter processes that are out of date and poorly maintained – covered in handwritten amendments, lacking version control, missing sections or entire pages. Unfortunately, this is usually an indication that the organisation does not take the management system seriously.

Poorly controlled processes place the operations they support – and by extension, the IMS and the wider organisation – at risk. Effective process control is a key requirement of any management system, and both certification and surveillance audits will involve a review of the processes that are pertinent to the parts of the IMS the auditor is examining. If the auditor finds that a process is out of date, for example, it may be considered a nonconformity.

The Standards do not require a specific format or method for the development of processes, and neither does this book. Every organisation develops and documents processes in its own way and there is little need for additional guidance on the practical side of doing so. Instead, treat these clauses as a prompt to implement the IMS in full and to ensure that your continual improvement process considers review, update and maintenance of key processes on a regular basis.

Leadership

Leadership is an essential driver in any organisation, and it is an essential component of a successful management system. Both ISO 27001 and ISO 22301 acknowledge this by dedicating Clause 5 to leadership and its related aspects.

Clause 5.1 of both standards provides a list of requirements that apply to the organisation's top management (i.e. the *"person or group of people who directs and controls an organisation"*).[11] They must establish appropriate top-level policies, ensure that the IMS is integrated into the organisation's operations, ensure sufficient resources for the IMS, communicate the importance of the IMS and of adhering to its requirements, ensure that the IMS achieves its goals, direct and support personnel to contribute to the effectiveness of the IMS, promote continual improvement and support other management roles as necessary.

Some of these requirements naturally lend themselves to delegation, such as providing resources or integrating the IMS into the organisation's operations. Others will likely happen naturally, such as supporting other management roles. For the remainder, top management will need to take a direct role in their delivery. Communicating the importance of cyber resilience and of complying with the IMS, for example, might be demonstrated by an all-staff briefing hosted by top management, while promoting continual improvement might be demonstrated by effective management reviews and regular staff communication regarding current nonconformities.

It is important to highlight that top management ultimately retains accountability for ensuring that the IMS achieves its intended goals. To fully realise that accountability, top management must have at least a basic understanding of the risks the management system is intended to address and the methods by which it will do so. This doesn't mean that top

---

[11] ISO 22301:2019 Clause 3.31.

management need to become information security or business continuity experts, but they may benefit from periodic training on common threats and vulnerabilities, business continuity fundamentals, etc.

There is no requirement to document the outcomes of this clause in either standard, so demonstrating to an auditor that the requirements are met usually involves discussions or interviews with members of top management. More mundane aspects such as whether the IMS is adequately resourced will often become clear to an auditor during the audit, but you might be asked to show invites to all-hands staff briefings or meeting minutes as evidence of communication, for example.

Policy

At the heart of any management system is a policy that outlines the high-level objectives the system is intended to achieve. ISO 27001 requires an information security policy, while ISO 22301 requires a business continuity policy.

Clause 5.2 in each standard addresses requirements for the policies in almost identical language. Each policy must be appropriate to the organisation's purpose, include management system objectives or a framework for setting those objectives, and commit to satisfy applicable requirements and continually improve the management system. The policies must be treated as documented information, communicated across the organisation and made available to interested parties on request.

It is important to note that top management must be the ones to establish these policies. Ideally, they should be involved in drafting them, as they will have the widest understanding of the organisation, the field it operates in, the legal requirements that may apply, and the scope and intent of the cyber resilience programme. They should also announce the policy to the wider organisation, both to emphasise how important it is to comply with the policy and the IMS, and to demonstrate top management's support for the overall programme.

One minor area of difference between the two standards is that ISO 22301 requires that the policy contain a framework for setting business continuity objectives, while ISO 27001 requires that the policy contain a framework for setting information security objectives or the objectives themselves.

A framework for setting management system objectives should broadly define who is responsible for setting objectives, how objectives will be selected, and how they will be monitored and reviewed. It is generally better for the policy to contain the framework rather than the objectives, as objectives tend to change more frequently than the framework they are based on.

Organisational roles, responsibilities and authorities

The last part of Clause 5 requires top management to assign roles and responsibilities for the IMS. Both standards ask that top management assigns the roles and responsibilities relevant to the IMS (such as IT security teams, incident response teams, internal auditors, and so on) and assigns responsibility for ensuring that the IMS meets the requirements of the standards. They must also assign responsibility for reporting on the performance of the IMS.

The specifics of the roles top management needs to assign will depend on the structure of the organisation and how you intend to implement the cyber resilience programme. Most organisations have an information security manager or a chief information security officer (CISO) whose skills and experience make them a natural fit to lead the project. If not, top management might opt to assign responsibility for the IMS as a whole or split it into separate domains (e.g. one person responsible for cyber security and another for business continuity).

If the scope of the IMS extends to multiple sites, top management will need to assign responsibilities for each site and determine how the sites coordinate. This will be particularly important for the business continuity side of cyber resilience, as each site will have different continuity risks.

Planning

Clause 6 begins with wording shared across both standards (albeit with slightly different numbering). Clause 6.1.1 requires the organisation to consider the internal and external issues and requirements of interested parties (identified under Clause 4), and identify the risks and opportunities that must be addressed to ensure the IMS does what it set out to do.

Once the risks and opportunities are identified, you must plan how to address them, decide how best to integrate any required actions into the processes of the IMS, and evaluate how effective those actions are. There is no requirement to treat any of the outputs of these actions as documented information, but you should consider how you might demonstrate to an auditor that these requirements are met, such as highlighting a potentially undesirable effect that was avoided or a risk to continual improvement that has been mitigated.

In both standards, the risks and opportunities referred to in 6.1.1 are those that affect the management system, not those that affect information security or business continuity. The goal of this clause is to design a better management system that fully accounts for the unique circumstances of the organisation. Risks and opportunities related to information security and business continuity are covered in later sections of the respective standard.

Information security risk assessment

At this point, the two standards briefly diverge. Clause 6.1.2 of ISO 27001 is one of the most important, as it defines requirements for information security risk assessment. These assessments are fundamental to the success of the ISMS (and by extension, the IMS) – you must understand the risks you face before you can mitigate them.

The organisation is required to define and apply an information security risk assessment process. This process must establish risk acceptance criteria (i.e. the level of risk the organisation is willing to tolerate) and criteria for performing assessments (i.e. a schedule or an assessment plan that ensures all areas of information security risk are periodically assessed).

There are many risk assessment methodologies that organisations can use, and neither standard mandates a particular one. ISO 31000:2018 *Risk Management —*

Guidelines, for example, provides general guidelines on risk management, while ISO 27005:2022 — *Information security, cybersecurity and privacy protection — Guidance on managing information security risks* offers guidelines specifically for managing information security risks. Either could be adapted to suit the organisation's needs, though the latter may be more immediately useful.

Whatever methodology your organisation uses, it must be able to identify risks to the confidentiality, integrity and availability of information, and it must provide consistent, valid and comparable results. It is therefore important that you select a risk methodology that can adapt to developments and changes in the risk landscape, as switching methodologies will inevitably result in discontinuities between historical results and current results. This is particularly important in a cyber resilience programme, as you face an ongoing need to remain ahead of – or at least, keep pace with – the state of the art in both attack and defence.

Confidentiality, integrity and availability are sometimes referred to as the 'CIA triad', and each information security risk should be assessed in terms of these three properties. Confidentiality risks might range from large-scale data breaches involving millions of records to an employee accidentally emailing a single file containing personal information to someone outside the organisation. Risks to integrity might include major data centre flooding that could wipe out entire databases or something as mundane as hardware failures in legacy storage media. Risks to availability could range from prolonged service outages arising from cyber attacks to losing the access code for the storage room containing archived paper files.

The risk assessment process should determine the level of risk by assessing the likelihood of the risk occurring and the impact on confidentiality, integrity and availability if it did occur. The output should be compared to the organisation's risk acceptance criteria, which will determine how the risk will be treated. Once identified and assessed, risks must be prioritised for treatment (usually on the basis of severity).

Finally, the risk should be assigned an owner. A risk owner is responsible for making sure that any treatments are implemented and that those treatments are effective. This means they must understand the process or activity affected by the risk, and the risk itself, to be able to judge whether a given treatment has achieved the intended result. They will also need the authority to make whatever changes to the process or activity are needed to treat the risk. In practice, this often means that operational or departmental managers are assigned as risk owners.

Each information security risk identified should be recorded in a risk register (often in a spreadsheet or dedicated risk management software). Once all risks are identified and assessed, they should be prioritised to ensure the most serious risks are tackled first.

The risk assessment process and risk register must be maintained as documented information. Risk registers are commonly maintained in spreadsheets or dedicated software for ease of use.

Information security risk treatment

Clause 6.1.3 of ISO 27001 is concerned with risk treatment. The organisation must develop an information security risk treatment process that selects appropriate treatment options based on the outcome of the risk assessment, and determines the controls needed to implement the selected treatment.

Risk treatment is commonly broken down into four options:

1. **Treat the risk** – apply controls to reduce the impact or likelihood of the risk so that the overall risk score falls within the risk acceptance criteria.
2. **Transfer the risk** – outsource the activity that leads to the risk to a third party that is better equipped to manage it, or purchase insurance to mitigate any potential impact.
3. **Terminate the risk** – stop doing the activity that leads to the risk, preventing any chance of the risk occurring.
4. **Tolerate the risk** – risks that fall within the organisation's risk acceptance criteria can be tolerated without treatment. However, they should be periodically reassessed to ensure that the risk remains within tolerable values.

Selecting suitable controls to treat an information security risk can be complex and depends heavily on the nature of the risk in question. Controls generally break down into four types:

1. **Organisational controls** (policies, processes, records, etc.).
2. **People controls** (training and skills, awareness, reporting, etc.).
3. **Physical controls** (physical locks, secure areas, CCTV, etc.).

4. Technological controls (Firewalls, anti-malware software, secure networking, etc.).

Annex A of ISO 27001 contains a representative list of information security controls categorised into these four themes, but you can also select controls from other information security frameworks or develop your own.

No matter which option you choose, you must compare the controls you select to those in Annex A to ensure that no necessary controls have been omitted. 'Necessary' in this context means 'relevant to the risks you have identified' – for example, if there are risks around transmission of data over the Internet, then encryption would likely be a necessary control.

This doesn't mean you have to implement every single control in Annex A, however. If your organisation does not develop its own software, then you would exclude controls related to secure development or access to source code as they do not apply. Similarly, if a given risk is effectively mitigated by another control, you do not need to add another from Annex A simply for the sake of it. However, you should review all the Annex A controls carefully with a view to cyber resilience, as there may be controls you can put in place now that protect against future risks that cannot easily be predicted.

Information about which controls you have and have not implemented and why must be recorded in a Statement of Applicability (SoA). The SoA must list all the controls in Annex A, together with the reason for their inclusion (or a justification for their exclusion) and their implementation status. If you develop additional controls or use controls from other frameworks, they must also be listed, along with the reason for their inclusion and their implementation status.

The SoA is one of the most important documents in your IMS, and it must be carefully maintained. It must be treated as documented information and periodically reviewed to ensure it remains up to date. If your organisation seeks certification for its IMS, the SoA will be a key area of focus for external auditors, so you should ensure it is readily available during audits.

Once you have identified the risks and defined treatment options and controls, the Standard requires that you develop a risk treatment plan. This should define the actions, responsibilities and priorities for implementing controls and evaluating their effectiveness. Risk owners must then approve the actions and controls (or suggest alternatives, if they feel the selected controls are unsuitable), and accept any residual risk that remains after treatment.

Like the risk assessment process, the risk treatment process must be treated as documented information. You may wish to consider treating the risk treatment plan itself as documented information as it is a key part of the ISMS side of the IMS. Note also that Clause 8.3 requires that the results of the risk treatment plan are maintained as documented information – this will naturally influence how you design the plan and the methods you select to evaluate risk treatment actions.

Information security and business continuity objectives

Both standards require that objectives are set for their respective management systems: information security objectives for ISO 27001 and business continuity objectives for ISO 22301. For both standards, objectives must be consistent with the ISMS/BCMS policy, be measurable (where practicable), account for any relevant requirements identified under Clause 4, and be monitored, communicated and updated. ISO 27001 also requires that information security objectives account for the results of information security risk assessment and risk treatment.

The objectives required are not objectives for the ISMS or BCMS – instead, they should describe high-level goals for information security and business continuity. An ISMS objective, for example, might be to reduce the number of information security events by a defined amount per year, while a business continuity objective might be to ensure no product or service is disrupted for longer than a defined duration.

When defining information security and business continuity objectives, you should consider how you will evaluate them. Not all objectives will lend themselves to easy measurement or evaluation, so you should consider possible methods before committing to an objective and avoid those for which evaluation would prove challenging. Objectives that cannot be measured or evaluated effectively are unsuitable and should be avoided.

Also unsuitable are objectives that do not have a direct relationship to information security or business continuity. 'Increasing year-on-year revenue' or 'improving value for shareholders' may be suitable business objectives, but they do not directly relate to either core subject, so certification auditors may consider them nonconformities.

Neither standard requires a specific format for objectives, but a common approach is to use the SMART format – specific, measurable, achievable, realistic and time-bound. Objectives for both parts of the IMS must be treated as documented information.

Planning changes

The last part of Clause 6 in both standards is about planning changes to the management system. ISO 27001 only requires that changes are carried out *"in a planned manner"*, but ISO 22301 goes further.[12] Alongside the same broad requirement as ISO 27001, the organisation must also consider the reason for the change and its expected outcome, the integrity of the management system, available resources, and any necessary allocation of responsibilities.

The difference arises because ISO 22301 was written under an older version of Annex SL (which, as noted earlier, defines the shared wording for all ISO management system standards). It is likely that updates to ISO 22301 will result in the wording of Clause 6.3 becoming aligned for both standards, but that may be some years away.

Nothing in either standard requires that there be a documented change process, records or documented information, so you have a good deal of leeway in how you approach this clause (though as always, be mindful of how you might demonstrate compliance to an external auditor). You could develop a single change management process

---

[12] ISO 27001:2022 Clause 6.3.

that accounts for the requirements of both standards, or separate processes for each component management system – or some other route entirely.

Readers familiar with ISO 27001 may know that Annex A includes change management as a technological control (A.8.32). The control refers to changes to information processing facilities rather than changes to the management system, so while there is some crossover, the control should be approached separately.

Support

Clause 7 in both standards is focused on supporting the IMS throughout its lifecycle. Organisations must provide resources, ensure the personnel working under the IMS are competent and aware of the IMS, manage internal and external communications related to the IMS, and manage documented information.

Resources

Both standards require that the organisation *"determine and provide the resources needed for the establishment, implementation, maintenance and continual improvement"* of the IMS. What this looks like will depend on which side of the management system you are looking at – the ISMS or the BCMS – so you should approach this as two separate tasks initially. Once you are confident that you have identified all necessary resources, you can compare the two outputs and check for overlap.

Resources for an ISMS might include IT hardware, software licences, services such as penetration testing or vulnerability scanning, or training expenses. The controls

3: Implementing cyber resilience

you implement to mitigate information security risks may come with their own resource requirements that must be managed, and you will need to consider budget for training and awareness measures to meet the requirements of subsequent parts of Clause 7.

Resources for a BCMS will likely be broadly similar, as the BCMS will use the organisation's IT systems and other standard functions and will need to provide training and awareness programmes. While it may be tempting to expand the remit of this clause to consider the resources you might need to manage and recover from disruptive incidents, such considerations should be left until the later parts of ISO 22301 that deal with business impact analysis (BIA) and incident response planning. Clause 7.1 is focused on the resources needed to operate and maintain the management system, not the resources needed to support information security or business continuity.

Competence

The success or failure of any project depends on the competency of those delivering it, and implementing cyber resilience with ISO 27001 and ISO 22301 is no exception. Clause 7.2 of both standards lists four requirements for competence:

- *"Determine the necessary competence of personnel doing work under its control that affects its information security (or business continuity) performance;*
- *Ensure these persons are competent on the basis of appropriate education, training or experience;*

- *Where applicable, take actions to acquire the necessary competence, and evaluate the effectiveness of the actions taken;*
- *Retain documented information as evidence of competence.* "[13]

These requirements refer to any personnel who affect the organisation's information security or business continuity performance. They are not limited to personnel with explicitly defined roles in the IMS, such as internal auditors or the person responsible for overseeing the management system. This doesn't mean that you suddenly need to provide training for the entire organisation, but it does mean that the process of defining and acquiring competence must account for the broader organisation as well as roles directly associated with the IMS.

It is for the organisation to determine the necessary level of competence. Although there is no explicit requirement for a documented process (only that evidence of competence is retained as documented information), you should consider developing a formal process to ensure that competency requirements remain consistent over time and that the effectiveness of training and related measures can be evaluated.

Competence does not necessarily equal training. An information security manager with a decade of experience likely has certifications, but also a good deal of practical knowledge. It is entirely acceptable for the organisation to

---

[13] ISO 27001:2022 and ISO 22301:2019 Clause 7.2.

deem someone competent based on experience alone, and this is often done for senior managers and other personnel who can demonstrate extensive knowledge and experience.

Personnel leading the project will naturally need a strong understanding of cyber security and business continuity and the skills to deploy ISO 27001 and ISO 22301 successfully. Qualifications such as Certified ISO 27001:2022 ISMS Lead Implementer or Certified ISO 22301 BCMS Lead Implementer might be sought if hiring, or provided if existing personnel do not have the requisite knowledge.[14]

Those with roles directly related to the IMS should understand their role and the purpose it serves in the IMS, and may need to acquire specific skills such as internal auditing or cyber incident response. Some roles will need greater familiarity with the two standards and their requirements than others, but at least a general understanding should be required for anyone working directly with the IMS.[15]

The organisation's remaining personnel will need to understand the processes, controls and other components of the IMS insofar as they relate to their immediate duties, but

---

[14] *https://www.itgovernance.co.uk/shop/product/certified-iso-270012022-isms-lead-implementer-training-course*, *https://www.itgovernance.co.uk/shop/product/certified-iso-22301-bcms-lead-implementer-training-course*.

[15] *https://www.itgovernance.co.uk/shop/product/certified-iso-270012022-isms-internal-auditor-training-course*, *https://www.itgovernance.co.uk/shop/product/cyber-incident-response-management-foundation-training-course*.

much of that will likely be achieved through internal training as the IMS becomes embedded in day-to-day operations, or through awareness briefings (which are covered in the next section).

Evidence of competence must be retained as documented information. This usually involves keeping copies of existing qualifications and certifications, documenting experience (where relevant) and keeping records of training courses completed by relevant personnel to aid evaluation. It is up to the organisation to decide how it wants to evaluate the effectiveness of actions taken to acquire competence, but questionnaires conducted after training, interviews, or more quantitative measures could be used.

Awareness

A successful management system is one under which every member of staff knows what the system is and what it is intended to achieve, how it affects their day-to-day tasks, and how their role contributes to its continuing effectiveness.

Clause 7.3 requires the organisation to ensure that personnel are aware of the IMS and their role in it. Both standards have the same core requirements, but ISO 22301 contains one extra.

Anyone working under the organisation's control (including contractors on your premises, temporary employees, etc.) must be aware of the information security policy and business continuity policy. It may be stating the obvious, but if personnel don't know about policies, they can't be expected to follow them.

They must also be aware of how they contribute to the IMS, why having an IMS is important, and what will happen (e.g. disciplinary measures) if they do not conform to the requirements of the IMS. Again, this may seem obvious, but even the most effective implementation may go over the heads of some employees simply because the IMS doesn't obviously affect their daily tasks. If all they notice is a small change in a process, they may dismiss the IMS (and by association, their role in it) as unimportant, then later fall foul of a more important requirement or take the wrong actions during a cyber incident.

The additional requirement unique to ISO 22301 asks that personnel understand the role and any responsibilities they have *"before, during and after disruptions"*.[16] This is essential for effective incident response but is another area where informal incident response plans, etc. often fall short, either by involving personnel who do not need to be involved (which usually just serves to complicate matters), or by neglecting to involve personnel who do.

A common approach to tackling this clause is to deploy staff awareness programmes, whether commercially available or developed in-house.[17] Commercially available programmes are usually fast, accessible and easy to deploy (usually using an elearning platform) but necessarily provide a generic overview instead of one customised to the organisation's specific circumstances. In-house-

---

[16] ISO 22301:2019 Clause 7.3 (d).

[17] *https://www.itgovernance.co.uk/shop/category/staff-awareness-e-learning-courses*.

developed materials avoid this issue but can be costly and harder to deploy.

There is no requirement for documented information in this clause, but depending on how you approach meeting the requirements, it is likely that you will have something you can show an auditor to demonstrate that an awareness programme is in operation (e.g. outputs from an elearning platform, meeting invites to awareness sessions, etc.).

There is also no defined frequency for conducting awareness training, but most organisations opt for annual sessions – anything longer would be ineffective and hard to justify. Certification auditors interview personnel about their awareness of the management system as a matter of course during audits, so refreshers can also be helpful.

Communication

There will be times in any management system implementation when the organisation needs to communicate something about the system to internal personnel or external entities. Both standards address this need in Clause 7.4, requiring that the organisation determines *"the need for internal and external communications"* relevant to the management system.[18]

This must include determining when and how to communicate, with whom, and what you will communicate. Because ISO 22301 does not yet align with the latest version of Annex SL (as discussed earlier), it also

---

[18] ISO 27001:2022 and ISO 22301:2019 Clause 7.4.

asks that the organisation determines who is responsible for communicating.

Neither standard asks for these communications to be managed by a formal process, and neither asks for documented information. A formal process would improve consistency and make responsibilities associated with IMS communications clearer, but some organisations may already have a system that achieves this. As always, if you do not opt for a formal process, consider how you might demonstrate compliance to an auditor.

Documented information

Clause 7.5 in both standards addresses 'documented information'. This refers to information that must be controlled for the management system to function effectively, such as objectives or key processes.

Requirements for something to be treated as documented information are throughout ISO 27001 and ISO 22301. However, the clause also requires that the organisation determines any additional information *"necessary for the effectiveness of the management system"* and treats that as documented information.[19]

How much additional documented information you need beyond the explicit requirements of the standards will depend on your organisation and how it operates. However, be strict about the 'necessary for effectiveness' test to avoid

---

[19] ISO 27001:2022 and ISO 22301:2019 Clause 7.5.1 (b).

spending time and effort controlling information that does not need to be controlled.

Clauses 7.5.2 outlines requirements for creating and updating documented information. 'Appropriate' identification and format are usually already accounted for by the organisation's base operating procedures and should require no special treatment (unless your organisation is in the habit of using obscure naming conventions or unusual document formats), but review and approval often involves extra legwork.

Most organisations review their policies and procedures from time to time, but this is frequently limited to a small number of critical documents and conducted in an ad hoc manner. The shift towards more frequent and extensive reviews required by a successful management system can require expectation management, and we highly recommend creating a review schedule – not just to improve planning, but also to ensure that all documented information that needs to be reviewed, is reviewed.

Clause 7.5.3 focuses on controlling documented information so it is available when it needs to be used and protected from loss of confidentiality or integrity, improper use and anything else that might render it unusable or incomplete.

To achieve this, the second part of 7.5.3 asks that the organisation addresses distribution and access, storage and preservation, change control, and retention as applicable. Distribution and access should pose little challenge as any functioning business has methods for ensuring that documents and files, etc. are available for use as needed. Change control essentially means tracking document version numbers so you can be sure the latest version is always in use. Storage, preservation and retention are likely to intersect with ISO 27001's Annex A controls on classification of information (A.5.12), protection of records (A.5.33) and information backups (A.8.13), and so may require more planning.

Controlling documented information can be achieved in a variety of ways, from a simple spreadsheet listing all documented information, their version numbers and date of last review, etc. to using software with built-in storage, version control and approval features like Microsoft SharePoint. In cases where hardcopy documented information is used for day-to-day operations, you should conduct periodic checks (e.g. as part of your internal audit programme) to ensure that the document is complete and that the latest available version is the one in use.

Finally, the organisation must identify and control documented information of external origin where that information is needed for the planning and/or operation of the management system. The nature of such information means it will need a slightly different approach to your own documented information – you may not have any control over version numbers or format, for example – but the number of affected documents is likely to be small. The first documents this will apply to are the two standards – ISO 27001 and ISO 22301 – you are using to implement cyber resilience.

Operation

Clause 8 is focused on implementing the processes needed to meet the requirements of each standard and integrating them into the organisation's existing operations. This clause contains some of the most important requirements for both the ISMS and BCMS.

Operational planning and control

Clause 8.1 requires that the organisation *"plan, implement and control"* the processes needed to meet requirements and achieve the actions determined in Clause 6 (i.e. actions to address risks and opportunities, determine objectives, plan changes, and for ISO 27001, developing the risk assessment criteria, assessment and treatment processes).[20] It is a prompt for the organisation to embed the IMS' processes in the broader operational context of the organisation and its day-to-day functions.

The organisation must define criteria for how it will control processes and apply that criteria to IMS processes. Suitable criteria might include regular checks to ensure that the latest process versions are being used, periodic reviews of relevant processes to ensure they reflect changes in the business or in how the processes are performed, assigning process owners and defining relevant responsibilities, etc.

The organisation must keep documented information *"to the extent necessary to have confidence that the processes have been carried out as planned"*.[21] What this looks like will necessarily be different for each organisation (and to some extent, which side of the IMS a particular process

---

[20] ISO 27001:2022 and ISO 22301:2019 Clause 8.1.

[21] ISO 27001:2022 and ISO 22301:2019 Clause 8.1.

falls on) – it might include automated logs, process outputs or other records.

The next part of Clause 8.1 requires that the organisation controls any planned changes to the management system and reviews any unintended changes. If an unintended change has adverse effects, the organisation must act to mitigate them. Although neither standard calls for one, it is usually easier to develop an IMS change management and review process to handle all three components.

Such a process should ensure that planned changes are checked by someone with the knowledge and skills to understand any potential impact on the IMS (usually the person with overall responsibility for maintaining it) and how those impacts could be mitigated. The same methodology used to determine the impact of planned changes can (in most cases) also be used to determine the impact of unplanned changes, so documenting at least that aspect is generally a good idea.

The last part of 8.1 is focused on supply chain management. ISO 27001 requires that the organisation controls *"externally provided processes, products or services that are relevant"* to the ISMS, while ISO 22301 requires that the organisation controls *"outsourced processes and the supply chain"*. [22]

The goal of these requirements is to ensure that outsourced processes, etc. that could affect the day-to-day operation of the management system, or the actions identified under Clause 6, are controlled in a similar manner to the processes

---

[22] ISO 27001:2022 and ISO 22301:2019 Clause 8.1.

the organisation will use to embed the IMS. Subject to the limitations of the relationship between you and the supplier, you can work with them to improve their processes, audit them to make sure that the processes being used are complete and the latest available, plan for alternatives should one supplier's process change so much that the product is no longer suitable, and so on. The important thing is to approach this with a mindset of process control to avoid overlap with the BIA and other key continuity processes.

Information security risk assessment and treatment

To be effective, information security risk assessment must be a cyclic process, not a one-off. Clause 8.2 in ISO 27001 recognises this by requiring the organisation to conduct information security risk assessments *"at planned intervals or when significant changes are proposed or occur; taking account of the criteria established in 6.1.2 (a)".*[23]

'Planned intervals' lets the organisation decide how often it should perform risk assessments, but most organisations do so at least annually. Longer gaps between assessments are difficult to justify because the threat landscape is constantly changing and new risks arise frequently. This puts the effectiveness of the management system at risk, and most certification auditors will consider any gap longer than a year insufficient.

Alongside significant changes, the criteria you develop should also define other scenarios that trigger a risk

---

[23] ISO 27001:2022 Clause 8.2.

assessment, such as suffering a data breach, identifying or being made aware of a new vulnerability that could affect the organisation's systems, acquiring a new subsidiary or working with a new supplier, or if a notable technical advancement occurs that might imperil existing security controls.

Clause 8.3 of ISO 27001 requires that the organisation implements the risk treatment plan. This usually takes place in a staged manner, beginning with the most serious risks and working back through severity levels until the treatment plan is fully implemented. This process should be subject to regular oversight to ensure it remains on track and to manage any unexpected difficulties.

For both 8.2 and 8.3, the organisation is required to keep documented information on the results. Your risk assessment process should provide for recording of results as a matter of course, so treating the outputs as documented information should not pose a problem. Similarly, your risk treatment plan should already define how you will evaluate the effectiveness of risk treatments, and the outputs of that process can be treated as documented information.

Business impact analysis and risk assessment

Clause 8.2 of ISO 22301 requires the organisation to implement and maintain *"systematic processes"* to analyse business impact and conduct risk assessments of potential disruptive events. Although it does not explicitly state that the BIA and business continuity risk assessment processes must be treated as documented information, they are central to the effectiveness of the BCMS and should always be controlled in line with the requirements in Clause 7.5.

The outputs of both the BIA and the business continuity risk assessment process must be reviewed at planned intervals, and after any significant change to the organisation or its operating context. These reviews are critical to the ongoing effectiveness of the BCMS, so it is important to schedule them and ensure the participants have the time to conduct them. Ideally, you should conduct the reviews before any management review so that top management can discuss any significant changes or new items at the management review meeting.

The BIA process

BIA is the process of identifying the activities your organisation performs to deliver products or services and understanding how each one could be affected by disruptive events. It allows you to identify the activities that must be prioritised to ensure an effective recovery and is one of the most critical procedures in the BCMS. For more in-depth information on the BIA process, ISO/TS 22317:2021 *Security and resilience — Business continuity management systems — Guidelines for business impact analysis* contains valuable guidance.

There is no avoiding the fact that BIA is a time-consuming and complex process, especially when performed for the first time during implementation. It is important to ensure that enough time and resources are available to conduct the BIA in a thorough and systematic manner, as the outputs of the process feed directly into development of continuity solutions and plans and strongly influence their overall effectiveness.

Impact types and criteria

The first step in the BIA process is to determine the types of impact the organisation could be subject to. This could include financial, reputational, contractual, operational, legal or environmental, in both direct and indirect forms. The outputs of the work done on the context of the organisation and the requirements of interested parties can help determine impact types.

The next step is to develop criteria for evaluating disruptive impacts. Although the specific types and criteria for impacts will differ depending on the nature of the organisation, the approach is generally the same.

When an activity is interrupted, there is a corresponding negative impact. The longer the interruption, the greater the impact. The criteria you are asked to define are the scale by which you evaluate a given type of impact, and it will be different for each type. Financial impact, for example, might be represented by a scale from £10 to £1,000,000 or more, while operational impact might be represented by a scale ranging from a few minutes of disruption to days, weeks or months.

Once you have developed appropriate impact scales for all applicable impact types, it can be helpful to consolidate the impact types and scales into a single matrix for ease of use. Although 8.2 makes no reference to documented information, the completed matrix should at least be subject to version control so you can ensure the latest version is used when conducting BIAs.

Identifying activities and assessing impact over time

Once you have a comprehensive impact matrix, the next step is to identify activities that support delivery of the products and services in scope of the IMS. This can be a time-consuming exercise and one that is prone to oversimplification, so it is important to take a systematic approach.

Identifying activities is best conducted in a visual format, in a similar manner to the way you would develop a data flow map. Beginning with a product or service in scope of the IMS, you can then draw a line to each process or activity that supports it, then to each process or activity that supports those processes, and so on until you have a visual flow that captures every single input and dependency into the product from beginning to end.

It is important that this process is comprehensive. You should approach this initial mapping stage on the basis that every activity connected to the product or service is relevant, even if there are several degrees of separation between them. You will determine which activities are critical and their priority later in the BIA process.

Repeat the mapping process until you have complete activity maps for all products and services in scope of the IMS. Where possible, involve the personnel who perform the activities you are mapping, as they can help you spot activities that might be missed or aspects in which the mapped activities diverge from actual practice.

The next step in the BIA process is to determine the impact over time that a disruption will cause to each of the activities identified in the previous step, using the impact scales you have developed. The impact matrix you developed earlier will help you determine which impact types apply; if an activity is subject to multiple impact types, you should determine the impact over time for all of them.

Impact over time is not necessarily linear. Some activities may have critical stages or thresholds at which a previously minor impact becomes major, perhaps as the result of a regulatory requirement or an operational factor. It is important to record any such spikes when determining impact over time, so you should ensure you are familiar with any externally imposed requirements or specific operational factors that result in them.

The completed impact profiles for each activity should be recorded and retained. You will need to refer to them (and re-evaluate them) in future BIAs, so it is good practice to keep them in an accessible format. As with the activity maps, you should consider at least applying version control so you can ensure use of the latest version and track any changes that occur in later BIAs.

Determine maximum tolerable period of disruption (MTPD)

Once you have impact profiles for your activities, you can determine the maximum tolerable period of disruption (MTPD). This is the point at which the impact of a disruption becomes unacceptable, irrespective of the reason. You can do this for each activity after you have plotted the impact profile or wait until you have profiles for all relevant activities (though the latter is often easier, as you can get all the relevant people in one place and work through several activities in the same session).

Some organisations define the MTPD by drawing an arbitrary line at a certain level of the impact criteria beyond which the impact is unacceptable, while some evaluate the various contributing factors and define a unique MTPD for each activity. Some MTPDs are imposed (or at least heavily influenced) by regulatory or contractual requirements; others are entirely up to the organisation. Some of the more peripheral activities in the activity map may not have an MTPD at all, or one that only occurs after such extended duration that it is rendered irrelevant by MTPDs applied to other, more critical activities.

There is no right or wrong way to determine MTPDs, and most organisations will use a combination of approaches. Try to avoid applying arbitrary MTPDs to all but the most peripheral activities and focus on applying the more detailed, holistic approach in a consistent manner. Documenting the methodology can help with this.

Determine recovery time objectives (RTOs) and minimum capacity

Once you have recorded MTPDs for all activities, the next step in the BIA process is to determine how quickly you must recover each activity to ensure the MTPD is not exceeded. This is known as the recovery time objective (RTO), and it must always be shorter than the MTPD.

When determining RTOs, you should first determine whether the activity can reasonably be recovered at full capacity, or if it will be necessary to recover it at partial capacity to avoid exceeding the MTPD. In most cases the goal is partial recovery, since full recovery of an activity may not be possible without exceeding the MTPD, and the organisation needs to get up and running as quickly as possible, even if that means operating at reduced capacity.

To help understand whether full or partial recovery is necessary (and to comply with the requirement in 8.2.2 (e) to resume activities at a *"specified minimum capacity"*), you must document the minimum operating capacity for each activity. This necessarily involves understanding the normal operating capacity of those activities – you cannot properly determine one without the other. Documenting the minimum capacity ensures you have a formal basis against which to design continuity plans and allows you to see, through testing and exercises, whether the plans deliver that capacity when put into action.

Some activities may allow for multiple levels of recovery capacity: a minimum, and subsequent greater levels that are still less than the normal capacity. Such cases may consequently allow for multiple RTOs, each associated with a different recovery capacity. Where this is the case, the strategies, solutions and plans based on them must clearly indicate which capacity (and RTO) is applicable to avoid confusion.

Recovery point objectives (RPOs)

RPOs are described in ISO 22313:2020 *Security and resilience — Business continuity management systems — Guidance on the use of ISO 22301* as a useful corollary to RTOs for activities that rely on data or information systems.[24] An RPO defines the amount of data you can afford to lose before you can no longer resume the activity (or put another way, the maximum acceptable period between backups). For example, if it would be impossible to resume an activity after more than 24 hours of data loss, then the RPO is 24 hours, and both the MTPD and the frequency at which backups of that data are created must be less than 24 hours.

RPOs are a useful tool to ensure that information is backed up frequently enough to allow an activity to be recovered. The same analysis used to define the RTO should also highlight the RPO where one is applicable, since you will need to understand the data necessary to perform the activity to be able to document the minimum operational capacity.

Identify prioritised activities

Once you have identified RTOs (and/or RPOs), you can begin to identify prioritised activities – the activities that must be completed (even if at a minimum capacity) to avoid an unacceptable level of impact during a disruption.

First, exclude all activities that the organisation does not need to recover during a disruption. You can then reorganise the remaining data to show RTOs in order of increasing length to develop a set of base priorities that you can later modify.

---

[24] ISO 22313:2020 is a useful resource for anyone implementing ISO 22301, whether standalone or as part of a cyber resilience programme.

RTOs are not the only consideration, however. In cases where several activities have the same RTO, one or more of those activities may be more crucial to maintaining the organisation's bottom line than the others and should therefore be prioritised. It may also be the case that an activity with a longer RTO needs to be prioritised over one with a shorter RTO to meet stakeholder or legal requirements.

These prioritised activities will play a major role in development of your business continuity plans (BCPs), so it is important to get this part of the BIA process right. Where factors other than RTO are relevant, you should record additional information so that the rationale for prioritisation is clear in future BIAs.

Identify resources and dependencies

Now that you have a complete list of prioritised activities, you can determine the resources each activity uses. Resources can include people (and any necessary skills or training, particularly those related to incident response); facilities or backup sites and utilities such as power, water and Internet connectivity; tools and equipment; IT systems and software; communication systems; products or services provided by suppliers and partners; and logistics. Your goal should be to develop a documented inventory of resources to help you track their use across the organisation's BCPs and make them easier to maintain over time.

Take care to identify resources that are shared across multiple activities (a common scenario with databases and other digital resources) and any that have a long lead time (particularly if the lead time exceeds the MTPD). It may be necessary to obtain long lead time resources in advance if it is not possible to obtain them fast enough to meet your defined recovery timescales. Resources provided by third parties, on the other hand, may be easy to acquire at short notice should it become necessary.

During implementation, there will naturally be support from top management for investment in recovery resources. However, the greater challenge is in maintaining them over the long term. Resources that go unused for long periods can be appropriated for more immediate needs and not replenished, and as the urgency of the implementation fades and is replaced by the day-to-day necessities of business, it gets harder to justify the expense of new resources needed to tackle new or changing risks.

There is no single way to mitigate this. The management review required by both standards will help keep the IMS in the minds of top management and other key decision-makers, and you should emphasise the benefits of the IMS and the cyber resilience programme when appropriate. Choose your battles carefully and justify any necessary expenses in positive terms rather than negative, as much as is possible.

The final factor in the BIA is to identify the dependencies on which the prioritised activities rely. This can be a complex task, especially in larger organisations with lots of concurrent activities, and you will need to refer to the activity maps you developed earlier in the BIA process.

Dependencies are activities that a prioritised activity cannot do without to function. Many of the more peripheral activities you identified during your activity mapping process will not be dependencies – anything that the prioritised activity does not expressly need should be excluded from this analysis.

Some dependencies may involve third-party products or processes. Where this is the case, you will need to consider how to maintain access during the period of disruption. This is especially important in scenarios where suppliers may themselves be disrupted.

In a cyber resilience programme, many dependencies will relate to data and digital processes. There may also be interdependencies where the same data or system is used in more than one prioritised activity. All this should be recorded, as it will heavily influence how you develop your strategies, solutions and business continuity plans.

Business continuity risk assessment

For your organisation to recover effectively from a disruption, you need to understand what kind of disruptive events you might face. ISO 22301 requires that the organisation has a defined risk assessment process (as per 8.2.3) to identify and analyse these risks and determine which risks require treatment.

Identifying business continuity risks can be more challenging than risk assessment in other management systems. Alongside more commonplace risks such as fire, flood or cyber attack, the organisation must also consider risks that are less likely but that can still result in a major disruption. This raises the question, especially for new business continuity practitioners, as to where to draw the line between risks that are genuinely out of scope and those that are unlikely but still relevant.

Relevant risks will arise in large part from the context of the organisation (and, to a lesser extent, the requirements of interested parties) and the nature of its operations. Most companies looking to implement a cyber resilience programme offer digital products or services of some kind, which naturally exposes them to more cyber continuity risks than (for example) a manufacturing organisation with a far more limited logical perimeter.

Attacks based on zero-day software vulnerabilities or newly discovered hardware vulnerabilities are far from common, but they cannot be reasonably excluded in the same manner as a London-based manufacturer might exclude the risk of a major earthquake. It is likely that you will end up with a subset of cyber continuity risks for which the outcome could be serious enough to warrant attention under the cyber resilience programme, but which cannot reasonably be predicted or defended against until they are discovered and publicised (or exploited by an attacker).

Despite being essentially impossible to fully plan for, many of the strategies and solutions you develop to manage more common cyber continuity risks will still be useful in tackling these outliers. They may, however, require a more flexible approach when developing business continuity plans, as it is much harder to predict what the specific impacts and effects of an unknown zero-day vulnerability might be.

Record the risks you identify in a risk register (which should be maintained as documented information) for ease of evaluation and so you have something to demonstrate to an auditor. You can then evaluate the likelihood and potential impact of each risk in line with the scale documented in your risk assessment process. If you are unsure about the mechanics and methodology of risk assessment, ISO 31000 provides a useful introduction, and there is a wealth of information available online.[25]

Business continuity strategies and solutions

Treatment for business continuity risks isn't based on applying controls, as you might expect for information security risks. Instead, ISO 22301 requires the organisation to develop strategies and solutions to tackle business continuity risks and recover prioritised activities.

8.3.1 requires that strategies consider *"options for before, during and after disruption"*, and notes that strategies *"must be comprised of one or more solutions"*.[26] Strategies are exactly what they sound like – the overarching strategic approach to treating one or more business continuity risks. Solutions are the specific actions needed to achieve a given strategy, and business continuity plans, which we will cover later, give effect to those solutions when a disruptive event occurs.

8.3.2 covers requirements for identifying strategies and solutions – essentially, a set of criteria for use in an identification process. Although a formal process is not called for, the identification, management and use of strategies and solutions is essential to the success of the

---

[25] ISO 31000:2018 *Risk Management – Guidelines*. Note that this standard is available for free at the ISO website: *https://www.iso.org/standard/65694.html*.

[26] ISO 22301:2019 Clause 8.3.1.

BCMS, so we recommend developing one that covers all of 8.3 (and treating it as documented information).

When faced with the prospect of a given disruptive event, it is natural to begin by considering a 'big picture' approach of how to respond. It is therefore usually easier to identify strategies first, focusing on the broad strokes of a particular disruptive event and how the organisation might respond. When identifying strategies, refer to the business continuity risk assessment, beginning with the most serious risks and working your way through until there is a strategy for all unacceptable risks.

Organisations are not restricted to a single strategy, and it is likely that some of the strategies you identify will be suitable for more than one risk. This is fine, though it will require care to avoid potential clashes when identifying solutions and developing business continuity plans. Avoid the temptation to identify potential solutions or delve into excessive detail at this stage of the process, as this can get in the way of strategic thinking.

Once you are satisfied with your strategies, you can consider potential solutions. This is one of the most time-consuming parts of the process during the implementation project, but it will get easier over time. Solutions are the actions that give effect to strategies, and each action in a strategy should be associated with one or more solutions.

Solutions must be specific. They define the steps the organisation will take to maintain the specified minimum capacity for prioritised activities in its BCPs, so they need to clearly capture what they are intended to achieve and how they will achieve it. This doesn't mean each solution needs to describe every step in minute detail – the BCPs that implement them during a disruption will do that – but they do need to contain enough information that someone knowledgeable can use them to develop a BCP.

When identifying solutions, it is better to cast a wide net. Not every potential solution you identify needs to be used, and some solutions that seem suitable at first may prove to be the opposite. The Standard does not expect you to 'get it right first time' – instead, testing and iteration are built into the management system to ensure improvement and weed out ineffective methods. Some solutions will be relevant to a wide range of business continuity risks (e.g. restoring backups), while others will only have relevance to a specific risk.

Once all strategies and solutions are identified, Clause 8.3.3 contains three requirements for selection: selected strategies and solutions should recover prioritised activities within the time frames and at the minimum capacity you have specified, take into account the organisation's risk appetite, and *"consider associated costs and benefits"*.[27] This latter requirement (to the relief of many a finance officer) embeds proportionality in the selection process – if the cost of a solution far outweighs the benefits, then alternative solutions should be considered.

With strategies and solutions selected, the next step is to determine the resources needed to implement the solutions. The list provided in Clause 8.3.4 is not exhaustive, and your process should ensure that all potential resource types are considered.

---

[27] ISO 22301:2019 Clause 8.3.3.

One of the most important aspects to account for is that some disruptive events may result in the need to deploy the same solution simultaneously in multiple places. This can impact the resources needed to successfully deploy the solution, particularly if it requires specific hardware or skills to function. Availability of expertise and personnel is an aspect often neglected during resource planning as we tend to assume that they will always be available – but if a disruptive event occurs while an employee with an essential skillset is on holiday, or if the event itself somehow renders them unable to perform the task, you suddenly have a much larger problem.

Suppliers are another important factor in resource planning. Solutions that rely on suppliers directly, or the products or services they provide, may require alternatives in scenarios where the disruptive event affects either the supplier or the organisation's access to the supplier's services. Tackling this usually involves building business continuity/cyber resilience due diligence checks into purchasing processes, evaluating current supplier continuity measures (e.g. via audits) and, where feasible, enforcing business continuity requirements through contracts.

The final requirement related to strategies and solutions is 8.3.5, which asks that the organisation *"implement and maintain"* the selected solutions so that they can be deployed should a disruptive event occur.[28] If costs necessitate a phased implementation process, begin with solutions that treat the most serious risks first and track

---

[28] ISO 22301:2019 Clause 8.3.5.

implementation progress so you can ensure nothing is missed or forgotten.

The organisation will also need to maintain its selected solutions. How this is done naturally depends on the type of solution in question, but you should consider developing a maintenance schedule to track the required actions and ensure they are completed.

Business continuity plans and procedures

Clause 8.4 of ISO 22301 deals with business continuity plans, procedures and actions associated with incident response. The organisation must develop a response structure to provide warnings and communication when an incident occurs and develop plans and procedures for responding to disruptions.

A BCP is essentially a structured list of procedures that deploy the solutions selected to respond to a disruption. It is worth noting that, throughout the Standard, references to BCPs are always in the plural. You are not expected to develop a single 'master plan' that addresses every possible disruption risk you have identified – in fact, it is almost always better to develop multiple BCPs, as doing so improves ease of use and allows for greater flexibility.

This doesn't mean you need a unique BCP for every single risk of disruption, however. It is perfectly acceptable (and entirely sensible) for BCPs to address multiple related disruption risks if the response procedures that will be used are the same or similar. As with so much about business continuity, the key is to strike a balance. If you find that adapting a given BCP to address a different disruption risk (or developing a BCP to tackle more than one) radically changes how the procedures are conducted, it is probably better to develop a standalone plan for that risk instead.

BCPs must be documented and must be based on the strategies and solutions you have selected. Clause 8.4.1 defines a set of requirements for the procedures that will comprise the BCPs, and you should ensure these are adhered to. In a cyber-resilience-focused IMS, these procedures will also need to address information security requirements related to the affected systems (e.g. restoring breached security controls or ensuring legal requirements are still met during the recovery process), which can prove challenging.

The requirement for flexibility can also be challenging, as procedures are usually developed to eliminate variance, not allow for it. One successful approach to tackling this is to build in 'check points' at key stages of the BCP, which call for the user to briefly pause, evaluate the scenario as it currently stands and seek additional guidance from senior personnel if needed. This kind of open-ended approach to flexibility is usually more valuable than trying to develop complex decision trees or if-then chains that govern what procedure should be used and when.

8.4.2 requires the organisation to set up a response team (or teams) that will be responsible for responding to a disruption. Roles and responsibilities within these teams must be defined and the team itself must have the knowledge and skills necessary to meet the requirements listed in 8.4.2.3 (which may require additional training in line with Clause 7.2).

The members of each team must be assigned alternates in case a team member is away or unavailable when a disruption occurs. These alternates need the same authority and skills as their counterparts to ensure they can perform the role adequately. Response teams also need documented procedures that cover the incident response process, from activation to communication, but these are covered in more detail in 8.4.4.

8.4.3 defines requirements for warning and communication. The organisation must develop procedures for handling and receiving communications (including with emergency responders and regional advisory systems), and for media response. It must also ensure that the means of communication remain available during a disruption and that the details of a disruption are recorded, including the actions and decisions taken when responding. Where applicable, the procedures should provide for informing parties that might be impacted by a disruption and for cross-coordination across multiple responding entities.

8.4.4 focuses on BCPs and associated procedures. BCPs are a core output of the BCMS, and if your organisation opts to certify its IMS, they will likely receive considerable auditor attention. Nonconformities in other parts of the IMS might not jeopardise the organisation's recovery, but nonconformities in the BCPs very well might, so it is essential that they are developed with care.

8.4.4.1 makes clear that BCPs must be documented, while 8.4.4.2 and 8.4.4.3 define a set of requirements that BCPs must contain. The first set of requirements apply 'collectively' across all BCPs, while the second set apply to each individual BCP. It may be sensible to create a short checklist that you can use to verify that BCPs contain all the necessary components before making them available for use.

Each BCP must be *"usable and available at the time and place at which it is required"*.[29] This is a particularly relevant consideration in a cyber-resilience-focused IMS, as it is likely that some of the potential disruptions the organisation faces will also result in electronic files and systems being partially or completely unavailable. Storing copies of BCPs in a third-party Cloud service is one option, but loss of Internet access would render this unavailable. Retaining hard copies of BCPs at all sites will always be the most secure option as it relies on no external component to function.

Although 8.4.4 calls for documented BCPs, it does not go as far as requiring them to be treated as documented information. It is difficult to see this as anything but an oversight – after all, 7.5.1 is clear that documented information requirements should apply to documents that are necessary for the effectiveness of the BCMS, and few things are as necessary to an effective BCMS as BCPs.

If it becomes necessary to respond to a disruption, you do not want to risk using an out-of-date or incomplete BCP. Treating BCPs as documented information will help ensure that the latest version is available and that the documents remain secure and protected.

---

[29] ISO 22301:2019 Clause 8.4.4.3.

Recovery

Clause 8.4.5 is concerned with recovering from a disruption. It requires that the organisation develops documented procedures to return to business-as-usual status following a disruptive event.

What these procedures will look like will depend on your organisation and its systems, services and products. Consider developing something akin to the BCPs you have already created – structured procedures that clearly define the actions, resources and responsibilities needed to restore normal functionality and capacity. For the same reasons as the BCPs, you should also consider treating the recovery procedures as documented information.

Exercise programme

The BCMS exercise programme is every bit as essential as the BCPs themselves. Clause 8.5 requires that the organisation implements and maintains an exercise and testing programme to validate the effectiveness of the selected strategies and solutions.

Clause 8.5 defines the requirements for the exercise and testing programme and is solely focused on strategies and solutions. However, it is important to note that Clause 8.4.3.2 requires that the warning and communication procedures defined in 8.4.3 must also be exercised as part of the programme.

The exercise programme should cover all strategies and solutions, along with warning and communications as applicable. The Standard calls for exercises and tests to be conducted at planned intervals and whenever the organisation experiences significant change; a typical programme might involve one or two larger exercises over a year, or more frequent but smaller exercises.

Exercises can range from full-scale reenactments to short tabletop exercises that examine only one or a small number of specific solutions. The results of exercises must be recorded in formal reports that highlight any issues and potential improvements, ensuring that the selected strategies and solutions continue to meet the organisation's needs.

The organisation is explicitly required to review and act on the outcomes of the exercise programme. If you opted to develop a formal change management procedure under Clause 6.3, then we recommend routing changes that arise from the programme through this procedure, as it will not only help ensure that the change is implemented properly but also provide useful evidence to show an auditor.

Evaluation of business continuity documentation and capabilities

The last of the clauses in the IMS that are unique to ISO 22301, Clause 8.6 requires that the organisation evaluates and verifies the suitability and effectiveness of BCMS documentation.

All the core BCMS documentation is included in this requirement, including the BIA, business continuity risk assessment, strategies and solutions, and BCPs and their associated procedures. The organisation is also required to evaluate supplier business continuity capabilities, and ensure its own documentation meets applicable legal and regulatory requirements. If changes are necessary as a result of these evaluations, they must be made in a *"timely manner"*.[30]

Much like the exercise programme, these evaluations must be conducted at *"planned intervals"* and after any significant change, but they must also be conducted after *"an incident or activation"* (of a BCP).[31] It may be helpful to build the post-incident reviews into the latter stages of the procedures you use to return to business as usual, to ensure they are conducted while the incident is still fresh in responders' minds.

Performance evaluation

Clause 9 in both standards addresses monitoring and measurement requirements. The data this provides will form the basis of your improvement programme.

The wording of Clause 9.1 differs slightly between the two standards, reflecting the differences in Annex SL across their respective publication dates and the differences necessary to address each management system. These differences are minor, and developing a system that works for both standards should pose little difficulty.

For example, both standards require that the methods used produce valid results, but ISO 27001 goes further and says that to be considered valid, the methods used should produce *"consistent and comparable results"*.[32]

---

[30] ISO 22301:2019 Clause 8.6 (e).

[31] ISO 22301:2019 Clause 8.6.

[32] ISO 27001:2022 Clause 9.1 (b).

Another minor difference is that ISO 27001 requires the organisation to evaluate information security performance and the effectiveness of the ISMS, while ISO 22301 requires evaluation of the performance and effectiveness of the BCMS. The former again reflects the version of Annex SL in use at the time of publication, but in practice, any monitoring and measurement system worth the name should account for both requirements easily.

The organisation is expected to maintain documented information as evidence of the results of monitoring and measurement, though there is no requirement for a documented procedure. However, ensuring consistent and comparable results without one will likely be difficult. Even if much of the monitoring and measurement is performed by automated IT systems, you will still need procedures for recording, interpreting and evaluating the outputs of those systems, and those procedures will need to be based on a defined methodology.

Given the importance of monitoring and measurement to the effectiveness of a management system, you may also consider that the methodology and associated procedures would fall within the remit of 7.5.1 (b) and so should be treated as documented information – but this is optional.

Clause 9.2 covers internal audits. These are common to all ISO management systems and are detailed, scheduled checks on whether the IMS continues to meet the requirements of the standards. ISO 22301's requirements are slightly more extensive than those of ISO 27001, but they both target the same goal. If there is no one in your organisation trained in auditing (which should be highlighted in the competence evaluations performed to meet 7.2 in both standards), you should consider Lead Auditor or Internal Auditor training.[33]

Clause 9.2.1 in both standards asks for internal audits at *"planned intervals"*.[34] Generally, certification bodies will expect that your audit programme encompasses all components of the management system over a year. Longer durations risk a critical nonconformity going unnoticed for long periods (this is particularly relevant to a cyber-resilience-focused IMS), and as such are unlikely to be considered sufficient.

Clause 9.2.2 focuses on the audit programme and audit methodology. For both standards, it is important to ensure that criteria and scope are defined for each audit, that objectivity and impartiality are maintained, and that audit results are reported to management. Certification body auditors will scrutinise the audit programme, so it is essential that all requirements are met (including that the programme itself and its results are retained as documented information).

ISO 22301 goes further by requiring that corrective actions are implemented *"without undue delay"* and that follow-up actions *"include the verification of the actions taken and*

---

[33] For example, IT Governance's Certified ISO 27001 Lead Auditor, Certified ISO 22301 Lead Auditor, and Certified ISO 27001 Internal Auditor training courses. For more information, visit: *https://www.itgovernance.co.uk/shop/category/iso-27001-training-courses*, and: *https://www.itgovernance.co.uk/shop/category/bcm-training-courses*.

[34] ISO 27001:2022 and ISO 22301:2019 Clause 9.2.1.

the reporting of verification results".[35] This is good practice for any audit programme, and to avoid the need to operate separate audit processes for each standard, it is simpler (and recommended) to treat these additional requirements as extending to ISO 27001.

Management reviews

Management reviews are another key part of the oversight processes built into ISO management systems. These are commonly conducted annually and give the organisation's top management an overview of the performance and effectiveness of the system(s) and an opportunity to drive improvement of the system as a whole.

Management reviews can pose challenges unrelated to the requirements of any standard. Top management tend to be very busy people, and finding a time slot of sufficient duration to complete a management review on a date that allows some or all members of top management to attend can be difficult. The data presented needs to be clear, concise and focused on the key issues rather than being bogged down in the day-to-day minutiae of running the IMS. It may be easier to schedule two management review meetings: one focused on the ISMS, and the other on the BCMS and the broader IMS.

The required inputs for management reviews are broadly similar across both standards, though each one has unique requirements that you will need to account for. Much like the audit programme, management reviews will be a key

---

[35] ISO 22301:2019 Clause 9.2.2.

area of focus during certification audits, so it is essential that every input and output in each standard is adequately addressed. In cases where there is no output (e.g. because there is no need for changes or improvements at that time), then it is usually sufficient to record this fact in the meeting minutes – you are not expected to generate extensive outputs if the inputs themselves do not require them.

The results of the management review (in both standards) must be maintained as documented information. This will likely take the form of documented meeting minutes and records of any actions deemed necessary by the review. In many cases, the actions can (and should) be fed into the IMS' continual improvement mechanisms, which will result in further documented evidence, should it be necessary.

Improvement

The final clauses of ISO 22301 and ISO 27001 diverge slightly, both in the detail of one of the requirements and in the order in which they are presented. To keep things simple, this book will address them in the order presented in ISO 22301, as it contains the more detailed requirement.

All ISO management system standards contain a requirement to manage nonconformities and corrective actions (10.1 in ISO 22301, 10.2 in ISO 27001). Any part of a management system that does not meet the requirements of the standard, either wholly or in part, is considered a nonconformity.

Nonconformities are often classified into two categories: minor and major. Minor nonconformities are usually understood to mean that the requirement in question is being met in part, but is missing some mandatory component – for example, you have information security objectives, but they are recorded in an uncontrolled document instead of being retained as documented information.

Major nonconformities are usually understood to mean that a requirement simply isn't being met at all, such as if you have no internal audit programme or BIA process, or where the deficiency is such that it completely undermines the objective of the requirement. In some organisations (including some certification bodies), major nonconformities can sometimes also be issued where there is evidence that minor nonconformities have not been addressed for extended periods, or where the same minor nonconformity recurs.

Many organisations and certification bodies also use a third category that, in the strictest sense, is not a nonconformity. These 'opportunities for improvement' highlight parts of the management system that, while meeting all the formal requirements of the standard, could be improved.

Both standards require the organisation to identify nonconformities, take corrective actions to resolve them, and identify the root cause so that other nonconformities arising from that cause can be identified and eliminated, and their recurrence prevented. Corrective actions must be reviewed to ensure they are effective, and both the nonconformities themselves and the corrective actions intended to resolve them must be retained as documented information.

Identifying the root cause is key to resolving nonconformities effectively. If you fail to identify and treat the root cause, there is a good chance the nonconformity will recur. Root-cause analysis is akin to detective work in that you must look beyond the immediate problem until you discover the true culprit.

Root-cause analysis requires a careful approach. There is often pressure to simply fix the current problem and move on, despite such an approach being essentially self-defeating (not to mention more costly), and personnel who perceive their role as unconnected to the nonconformity (even when it turns out that an action they take later results in a nonconformity elsewhere) can react poorly to what they see as 'being investigated'.

If you are approaching root-cause analysis for the first time, there are several techniques you can use, many of which were developed for quality management. A simple one is 'five whys': you begin with 'why did the nonconformity happen', and once you have the answer, then ask 'why did that happen?', and so on until you get to the source. 'Five whys' got its name because it usually takes around five 'whys' to reach the root cause, although the number will vary depending on the nonconformity.

The great majority of nonconformities and corrective actions will arise from your internal audit programme and, if the organisation seeks and achieves certification, through audits by certification bodies. However, they may also be identified through day-to-day interactions with the management system, particularly by personnel responsible for the IMS or parts of it, and so your continual improvement programme should allow for any staff member to suggest potential improvements or flag up potential nonconformities.

With continual improvement in mind, both standards contain a broad requirement for continual improvement (10.2 in ISO 22301, 10.1 in ISO 27001). The core requirement is identical in both standards – the organisation must *"continually improve the suitability, adequacy and effectiveness of the management system"*.[36] The absence of any requirement for formal processes, records or methodologies leaves this entirely to the organisation to define, and many organisations already have improvement mechanisms in place that can be adapted for this purpose.

Such mechanisms tend to be either light-touch, informal systems or more complex, formal ones. In an IMS based on ISO 22301 and ISO 27001, a more complex, formal mechanism is likely more appropriate, as ISO 22301 also requires that the organisation considers *"the results of analysis and evaluation, and the outputs from management review, to determine if there are needs or opportunities, relating to the business, or to the BCMS, that shall be addressed as part of continual improvement"*.[37] If seeking certification, it will be necessary to demonstrate that this part of the requirement is met, and an easy way to do that would be to point to the sort of records generated by a more formal system.

ISO 27001 Annex A

Annex A of ISO 27001 contains 93 information security controls, categorised into 4 themes:

---

[36] ISO 22301:2019 Clause 10.2 and ISO 27001:2022 Clause 10.1.

[37] ISO 22301:2019 Clause 10.2.

- Organisational (37 controls)
- People (8 controls)
- Physical (14 controls)
- Technological (34 controls)

As noted earlier, the information security risk assessment and risk treatment plan will largely define the controls you choose to implement, but you should also review the full list of controls in detail with a view to cyber resilience over the longer term, as there may be relatively simple preventive controls you can implement to guard against risks you cannot reliably foresee. It is all but impossible to predict a new zero-day vulnerability, but you can protect against at least some of them by implementing organisational, technological and other controls that may otherwise seem superfluous.

This book will not cover all controls in detail, as doing so would easily double its size while adding little value. Instead, it will take a brief look at some Annex A controls that are particularly relevant from a cyber resilience perspective.

Organisational

Within the organisational controls category, 'contact with special interest groups' (5.6) aligns with the need to keep up to date on the latest threats, vulnerabilities and attack techniques so you can better defend against them and mitigate them should they occur. 'Information security in project management' (5.8) also contributes to resilience by ensuring that security is considered during new projects and product development.

5.20 and 5.21 cover information security in supplier agreements and managing security across the ICT supply chain. Both are essential for effective resilience: you must address information security (and continuity) in agreements with your suppliers, particularly those that supply key components or that provide resources used in your business continuity plans.

5.24 covers incident management and preparation. In a cyber-resilience-focused IMS based on ISO 27001 and ISO 22301, at least part of this control will likely be met by your business continuity planning, BCPs and other related materials. Similarly, 5.25, 5.26 and 5.27 on assessing and categorising information security events, and responding to and learning from information security incidents will share some ground with the business continuity side of the IMS, but only a subset of information security incidents will impact the organisation's continuity or require that BCPs, etc. are activated, so the processes associated with these controls will need to reflect that.

The relevance of maintaining information security during an incident (5.29) and on ensuring ICT readiness for business continuity (5.30) should require little explanation. While the latter will tie heavily into the business continuity side of the IMS, the former will need to be embedded both in BCPs and in the procedures used to address incidents that do not impact continuity.

People

Of the controls in the 'people' category, only two are of immediate relevance to the practical aspects of cyber resilience (though the others remain valuable, of course).

Security of remote working (6.7) and security event reporting (6.8) both need to be considered in detail to achieve effective cyber resilience. Remote working expands the logical perimeter of the organisation beyond traditional boundaries and requires security measures suited to the task, but it can also play a significant role in maintaining business continuity during a disruption and for some organisations, can constitute a solution in its own right.

Having a mechanism for employees to report any suspicious behaviour or possible attacks is a critical component of any resilience programme. Automated event monitoring systems have made great strides in recent years and can be extremely effective, but by definition, they can only look at digital events.

Human beings, on the other hand, are often very alert to minor changes in the systems they use, the tasks they perform and the people they interact with, and play an important role in maintaining physical security as well as digital. A costly SIEM system can only detect an attack stemming from a 'lost' USB drive found outside the premises once it is connected and an attack has begun; a person with good cyber security awareness can report the drive to the IT team for proper investigation before it ever touches a USB port. While cyber resilience is as focused on surviving a successful attack as it is preventing them, prevention remains the best medicine.

Physical

A few physical controls stand out. Protecting against physical and environmental threats such as fires, floods, heatwaves, etc. (7.5) is an essential part of business continuity risk management, and protecting off-site assets (7.9) such as backup IT infrastructure that form part of your business continuity solutions is also important. Supporting utilities (7.11), cable protection (7.12) and equipment maintenance (7.13) all contribute to more secure and efficient infrastructure and therefore support your continuity efforts.

Technological

Almost all the technological controls have a role to play in cyber resilience. This is because a cyber resilience programme presupposes a strong baseline level of security to better focus strategies, solutions and BCPs on the more intractable risks instead of wasting effort surviving attacks that could easily have been prevented. However, there are a few that have more immediate relevance to the programme.

Malware protection (8.7), regular vulnerability scanning and penetration testing (8.8) all play an essential role in achieving and maintaining that baseline level of security, helping you defend against common attack vectors and highlighting potential weaknesses before an attacker can take advantage.

Capacity management (8.6) will naturally form a key part of your business continuity solutions and BCPs, but while the Annex A control focuses solely on digital capacity, in a cyber-resilience-focused IMS it is important that continuity strategies and solutions also provide for sufficient capacity in personnel, sites, utilities and other resources. In a similar vein, ensuring information processing facilities have sufficient redundancy to meet availability requirements (8.14) should be applied not just to the information systems in those facilities, but also to the utilities, personnel and resources that support the function of those systems and facilities.

The role that backups (8.13) play in recovery and resilience needs no explanation, but the need to ensure that it is possible to restore lost data in the time frames defined in your recovery point objectives may force changes to existing systems that cannot meet those requirements. It is also important to consider continuity requirements for the backups themselves – if they are all held locally on site, for example, then disruptive events may affect them every bit as much as the main facilities.

CHAPTER FOUR: CERTIFICATION

Although ISO publishes both standards, it does not offer certification services. Instead, local certification bodies are accredited by national accreditation bodies to evaluate management system conformity and issue certificates.

In the UK, accredited certification schemes are managed by UKAS. In the US, the equivalent body is ANAB. However, it is important to note that there is no legal requirement for a certification body to be accredited. This results in two unofficial 'tiers' of certification: those that are issued by accredited certification bodies, and those that are not.

Accredited certification is valuable because the certification body has been independently assessed as competent to evaluate the management system in an impartial and objective manner. As a result, certificates issued by an accredited certification body are recognised by suppliers, partners and other accreditation bodies around the world as a valid, independent determination of conformity.

Unaccredited certification offers no such confidence. Without independent verification of the certification body, organisations have no way to know whether the certification body is applying the standard correctly, so the certificate means very little. A certificate from an unaccredited certification body will be an immediate red flag to practitioners, as the unspoken assumption is that the organisation will not or cannot achieve certification from an accredited body, and therefore that the management system is deficient.

If a customer or partner asks that you achieve certification to an ISO standard (no matter which one), they will almost always be referring to accredited certification. It would generally be unwise to secure certification from a certification body that is not accredited by UKAS or by another national accreditation body. Similarly, if you need assurance from a supplier, you should check that any certification they provide is also from an accredited certification body.

The certification process

Certification is usually a two-stage process involving independent audits conducted by the external certification body. Depending on how you have developed your IMS and the availability of personnel at the certification body, this may involve two auditors (one to review each 'component' management system, perhaps on different visits) or just one (if someone with appropriate skills and training for both is available).

The initial audit will focus on whether you are implementing the IMS correctly and in line with the standards, and will examine various key requirements to ensure they are being met. Do not worry if the auditor discovers nonconformities at this stage – this is common, and the auditor will use them as an opportunity to help you better understand the requirements and how they should be applied.

After the first audit, you will have a clear idea of where you are meeting requirements and where you are falling short.

You can then develop an action plan to implement any necessary changes in preparation for the certification audit.

The certification audit will examine the various constituent parts of the IMS to ensure they meet requirements. The auditor will look for evidence that the IMS is implemented, functional and operating effectively, which will likely involve reviewing the BIA and BCPs, the information security risk assessment, the risk treatment plan and the Statement of Applicability, alongside evidence of audits, management review, objectives, etc.

The goal should be to begin the certification audit with confidence that there are no major nonconformities in the IMS. A small number of minor issues noted can usually be resolved through your continual improvement process in agreement with the certification body, but any major nonconformities identified will likely result in the certification body refusing to issue certification until they are resolved to its satisfaction.

Maintaining certification

Once you have achieved certification, you then need to maintain it. Most accredited management system certificates are valid for three years, during which you will be subject to surveillance audits by the certification body.

Surveillance audits are usually conducted twice annually. Each audit will examine different aspects of the management system so that the entire management system is independently reviewed by the time the certificate is due to expire. Members of top management should be present for surveillance audits, as they will be expected to be able to demonstrate knowledge of the IMS and its objectives, adherence to the leadership requirements and overall responsibility for the system.

Minor nonconformities identified during surveillance audits are generally left for the organisation to resolve on its own, though auditors will generally expect that they are resolved and closed within three months (or within the time frame agreed with the certification body).

If a major nonconformity is identified, the certification body will often ask that you develop a formal corrective action plan. This will describe in detail how you will resolve the nonconformity and set a time frame for completion to be agreed with the certification body.

Recertification

Towards the end of the certificate's lifespan, you will undergo a recertification audit. This will be similar to the certification audit and will examine your IMS in detail, with additional focus on the effectiveness and performance of the system as implemented. At the conclusion of the audit, the lead auditor will make a recommendation to the certification body in respect of your recertification.

Minor nonconformities identified during the recertification assessment are unlikely to affect the lead auditor's recommendation, unless they are in large numbers or are indicative of a more significant problem. If any major nonconformities are identified, however, it is likely that the lead auditor will not recommend that your certification is renewed until they are resolved.

If this occurs, you will need to agree a formal corrective action plan with the certification body (as described earlier). If the nonconformity is not resolved, or the second recertification audit reveals further major nonconformities, then your certification will almost certainly be suspended or revoked.

The final decision always rests with the certification body. Most certification bodies permit the organisation to dispute the findings of a third-party auditor, but you should be very sure of your ground before making a complaint.

Maintaining resilience

Much of this book has, by necessity, focused on how to meet the requirements of the two standards as a route to implementing a cyber resilience programme. Implementing the programme, however, is only the first step. Once it is established, you must maintain the programme and stay resilient, otherwise all your work will go to waste.

Maintaining resilience isn't easy. Like Alice racing the Red Queen, you must run as fast as you can simply to stay in place – and you are not just racing your attackers: you must also race against the organisation's own inertia.

All too often, cyber resilience programmes (and management systems in general) are implemented with much fanfare and acclaim, only to then suffer a slow decay into irrelevance. Accredited certification offers guardrails against this, as falling too far from the requirements of the standard risks costing you the certification. Yet even within those guardrails, there is room for systems and controls to slowly become less effective. Financial and operational priorities shift, roles and responsibilities change and are reallocated, expertise is lost and gained through natural staff turnover, and core technologies change over time – all of which imperil the organisation's resilience.

Pushing back against this inertia is challenging and is part of the reason top management support is so essential – not just during the implementation, but over the long term. Without it, you face an uphill battle to maintain relevance, which usually culminates in a less effective system and consequently weakened resilience.

There is no one right answer to tackling this problem. Solutions are necessarily unique to the organisation, the personalities and roles within it, and the business environment in which it operates. Maintaining (at least annual) cyber security and resilience briefings for top management, conducting regular cyber security awareness training for all staff, and ensuring the organisation retains personnel with key cyber security and resilience skillsets can all help keep your resilience programme active and efficient, but ultimately you will have to decide how best to keep your organisation on track.

Of course, while you are doing these things, your attackers are sharpening their virtual knives and probing for weaknesses in your defences. It is essential that you keep abreast of current developments in the field through cyber security news sources, reputable threat assessment reports and best-practice advice published by agencies such as the UK National Cyber Security Centre (NCSC), the European Union Agency for Cybersecurity (ENISA) or the National Institute of Science and Technology (NIST) Computer Security Resource Centre in the US.

Investing in SIEM systems and other technical measures that automate and centralise the more mundane technical aspects of cyber security can be valuable, but not all organisations have the budget for these more elaborate solutions. For these organisations, even greater emphasis should be placed on process and people risks, with regular refreshers and updates when changes occur.

Regular penetration testing and vulnerability scanning can help you stay ahead of newly identified vulnerabilities, and building cyber security into the design phases of product and service development also goes a long way in maintaining a strong base level of resilience. Regularly testing your business continuity plans and keeping the strategies and solutions they rely on up to date (not to mention regularly reviewing and updating the BIA), and gradually extending business continuity and cyber resilience requirements to your suppliers all contribute to maintaining resilience.

Like Sisyphus and his boulder, the task of maintaining effective cyber resilience never truly ends. But with foresight, strategic planning and engagement, you can defend against the expected and survive the unexpected.

Third-party resilience

According to Verizon's 2024 Data Breach Investigations Report, supply chain influence in data breaches increased from 9% in 2023 to 15% in 2024, a year-on-year increase of 68%.[38] Major supply chain compromises such as 3CX and SolarWinds leveraged weaknesses in those companies'

---

[38] Verizon, *2024 Data Breach Investigations Report*, 2024, https://www.verizon.com/business/resources/reports/2024-dbir-data-breach-investigations-report.pdf.

software development processes, resulting in massive impacts that affected millions of customers, including the US federal government.[39] Awareness of the need for supply chain information security is rising, but continuity is an equally important consideration.

Supply chain cyber security and continuity are essential components of cyber resilience because a great many organisations allow suppliers to connect to their systems (or vice versa). This results in holes in the organisation's logical perimeter that, for all the supplier's good intentions, can be exploited by any attacker who successfully compromises the supplier. Even organisations that don't allow suppliers direct access to their systems can still be attacked through a supplier if the products or services it supplies to the organisation are compromised, and any organisation that relies on a supplier for key products or services can be disrupted if the supplier is itself disrupted.

Extending business continuity and cyber resilience requirements to your supply chain can be challenging. It is all very well for standards to ask for changes to contracts and agreements that extend your resilience and continuity requirements to your suppliers, but the real world is rarely so accommodating.

The influence an organisation can bring to bear when asking suppliers to meet new conditions tends to be proportionate to its size, market reach and purchasing power. Smaller organisations cannot realistically expect to

---

[39] Verizon, *2024 Data Breach Investigations Report*, 2024, https://www.verizon.com/business/resources/reports/2024-dbir-data-breach-investigations-report.pdf.

impose requirements on larger organisations unless those requirements are something the larger is already doing or plans to do, and in many cases, there is little point in even trying. A small or medium enterprise of a hundred or so employees is not going to be able to convince Amazon Web Services (AWS) to change its Cloud services to align with the SME's continuity requirements – it must either accept what AWS does now and take its own steps to remedy deficiencies in areas over which it does have control, or seek another provider.

As a result, when it comes to ensuring cyber resilience and continuity in your supply chain, while you should use the organisation's influence in a positive manner when you can, you must also accept and manage the great many situations in which you cannot. Sometimes the latter means changing how your organisation does things to reduce or mitigate a potential supplier vulnerability, while sometimes it means moving to another supplier entirely – and even in those cases, you may still need to take extra steps during any transition period.

For suppliers that you can influence, dialogue is key. Small and medium-sized suppliers are often willing to engage in discussions about potential improvements, but few people (or organisations) respond favourably to a demand. Cultivating good relationships with key suppliers and approaching discussions of cyber resilience with tact and humility can go a long way to smoothing the road, and you can point to any number of high-profile supply chain compromises in the media to illustrate the (very real) risks. Consider ways you can offer support – whether financial, expertise, or otherwise – so that it feels less like an imposition and more like a collaboration.

For further guidance on supply chain management for business continuity, consider purchasing ISO/TS 22318:2021 *Security and resilience — Business continuity management systems — Guidelines for supply chain continuity management.*

CONCLUSION

If you have got this far, you are now prepared to use ISO 27001 and ISO 22301 to implement a cyber resilience programme. Reading this book, however, is the easy part. Implementing cyber resilience is a challenge in any organisation, and requires planning, focus, resources, continual improvement, and above all, top management support throughout the project.

If it is done properly, your organisation will be better protected than ever – and just as importantly, it will have clear plans and solutions for responding to successful cyber attacks and disruptions, should they occur. No matter what the future holds, you can help your organisation protect, defend and survive.

FURTHER READING

GRC Solutions is the world's leading publisher for governance and compliance. Our industry-leading pocket guides, books and training resources are written by real-world practitioners and thought leaders. They are used globally by audiences of all levels, from students to C-suite executives.

Our high-quality publications cover all IT governance, risk and compliance frameworks and are available in a range of formats. This ensures our customers can access the information they need in the way they need it.

Other books you may find useful include:

- *Digital Ethics in the Age of AI – Navigating the ethical frontier today and beyond* by Dr Julie Mehan, *https://www.itgovernance.co.uk/shop/product/digital-ethics-in-the-age-of-ai-navigating-the-ethical-frontier-today-and-beyond*
- *IT Governance – An international guide to data security and ISO 27001/ISO 27002,* Eighth edition by Alan Calder and Steve Watkins, *https://www.itgovernance.co.uk/shop/product/it-governance-an-international-guide-to-data-security-and-iso-27001iso-27002-eighth-edition*
- *NIST CSF 2.0 – Your essential introduction to managing cybersecurity risks* by Andrew Pattison, *https://www.itgovernance.co.uk/shop/product/nist-*

csf-20-your-essential-introduction-to-managing-cybersecurity-risks

For more information on GRC Solutions and IT Governance™, a GRC Solutions Company as well as branded publishing services, please visit *https://www.itgovernance.co.uk/*.

Branded publishing

Through our branded publishing service, you can customise our publications with your organisation's branding. For more information, please contact:

clientservices-uk@grcsolutions.io

Related services

GRC Solutions offers a comprehensive range of complementary products and services to help organisations meet their objectives.

For a full range of resources, please visit *www.itgovernance.co.uk*.

Training services

GRC Solutions' training programme is built on our extensive practical experience designing and implementing management systems based on ISO standards, best practice and regulations.

Our courses help attendees develop practical skills and comply with contractual and regulatory requirements. They also support career development via recognised qualifications.

Learn more about our training courses and view the full course catalogue at

www.itgovernance.co.uk/training.

Professional services and consultancy

We are a leading global consultancy of IT governance, risk management and compliance solutions. We advise organisations around the world on their most critical issues and present cost-saving and risk-reducing solutions based on international best practice and frameworks.

We offer a wide range of delivery methods to suit all budgets, timescales and preferred project approaches.

Find out how our consultancy services can help your organisation at

www.itgovernance.co.uk/consulting.

Industry news

Want to stay up to date with the latest developments and resources in the IT governance and compliance market? Subscribe to our Security Spotlight newsletter and we will send you mobile-friendly emails with fresh news and features about your preferred areas of interest, as well as unmissable offers and free resources to help you successfully start your project: *www.itgovernance.co.uk/security-spotlight-newsletter.*

EU for product safety is Stephen Evans, The Mill Enterprise Hub, Stagreenan, Drogheda, Co. Louth, A92 CD3D, Ireland. (servicecentre@itgovernance.eu)

www.ingramcontent.com/pod-product-compliance
Lightning Source LLC
Chambersburg PA
CBHW042315210326
41599CB00038B/7133